# Systematic Theology for Kids

*What the Bible Says About God, Jesus, Sin, and Salvation—Explained Simply for Children*

# TABLE OF CONTENTS

# INTRODUCTION
## START YOUR SEARCH FOR TRUTH

You stand on the starting line. Your heart beats fast. You want to win the game. You want to play your best. But you cannot just run onto the field without a plan. Every great athlete spends hours studying the playbook. They know the rules. They know where their teammates will be. They know what the coach expects. If you want to succeed in your sport, you have to know the facts. The same is true for your life with God. You need to know the truth about who he is and how he wants you to live.

Do you know what makes a great athlete? Discipline and knowledge are the keys to success. You do not just guess how to throw a ball or run a play. You learn the right way to do it. This book is like your spiritual playbook. It helps you organize what the Bible says so you can live with confidence. Some people think the Bible is just a collection of old stories. It does have many stories, but they all fit together into one big message. That message is what we call theology.

## What Is This Big Word?

The word "theology" sounds like something for people in long robes. It sounds like something for people who spend all day in a library. But theology is actually very simple. The first part, "theo," means God. The second part, "logy," means the study of something. So, theology is just the study of God. Systematic theology is a way to organize that study. It is like a gear bag for your mind. You do not just throw your cleats, your jersey, and your water bottle into a messy pile. You put them in specific spots so you can find them when the game starts.

When we look at the Bible systematically, we put topics together. We look at everything the Bible says about God the Father in one place. Then we look at everything it says about Jesus. We do this with sin and salvation too. This helps us see the big picture. It stops us from getting confused. If you only look at one verse here and one verse there, you might miss the point. But when you see how everything fits together, the truth becomes clear. This book helps you build a solid foundation.

## Why Truth Matters

You live in a world with a lot of noise. People have many different opinions about God. Some people say he is just a feeling. Others say he is a judge who waits for you to fail. Some say he does not exist at all. If you do not know the truth, you will get tossed around like a ball in a windstorm. You need to know what is real. In sports, the rules do not change based on how you feel. A foul is a foul, whether you like it or not. The truth about God is the same way. It is steady and firm.

Why do we need to organize our thoughts about God? We do this because the Bible is big and we want to see how the pieces fit together. When you understand the truth, it changes how you play. It changes how you treat your teammates. It changes how you act when you lose a game. Knowing God gives you a reason to play that is bigger than a trophy. It gives you a purpose that lasts longer than a season. You are not just playing for yourself. You are playing for the one who created you.

## The Four Main Sections

We have broken this search for truth into four sections. Each one focuses on a big part of the Bible.

- **Section 1: Know Your Holy Creator.** Everything starts with God. Before there were stars or oceans or soccer fields, there was God. We will look at who he is and why we can trust his Word.

- **Section 2: Follow the Living Savior.** This section is all about Jesus. He is the hero of the story. We will see why he came to earth and what he did for us.

- **Section 3: Face the Problem of Sin.** This is the tough part of the playbook. We have to talk about what went wrong. Sin is like a major injury that keeps us out of the game. We need to know how serious it is.

- **Section 4: Join the Great Rescue.** This is the best part. It tells us how God brings us back to him. It explains how you can have a new life and a new goal.

## How to Use This Playbook

You do not have to read this book all at once. You can take it one chapter at a time. Each chapter is short and direct. We use the New Standard Version (NSV) for Bible phrases. This helps keep the language clear. As you read, think about your own life. Think about your team and your school. How does the truth about God change your day?

Can a kid really understand big ideas about the Creator? Yes, because God made the truth plain enough for everyone to see. You do not need to be an adult to know the Lord. You just need to be willing to listen. God wants you to find him. He is not hiding. He has given us his Word so we can know exactly who he is.

## Getting Your Mind in the Game

Training your mind is just as important as training your body. You lift weights to get strong. You run sprints to get fast. Reading this book is training for your soul. It builds your faith so you can stand strong when life gets hard. When you know the truth, you have a solid place to stand. You will not be tricked by lies. You will know your Coach, and you will know the plan.

The Bible says that the truth will set you free. That means you do not have to worry about being "good enough" on your own. You do not have to guess what God wants. He has already told us. Your job is to study the playbook and get ready to move. This is the most important search you will ever go on. It is not about finding a hidden treasure. It is about knowing the person who made the treasure in the first place.

## The Goal of Our Study

The goal is not just to know facts. If you know all the rules of baseball but never pick up a bat, you are not a player. You are just a fan. We do not want to be fans of God. We want to be his followers. We want to be on his team. This study should lead you to love God more. It should make you want to talk to him in prayer. It should make you want to help others.

True theology leads to a life of action. It makes you a better friend. It makes you a harder worker. When you see how much God loves you, you cannot stay the same. You want to give him your best effort in everything you do. Whether you are on the court, in the classroom, or at home, you are representing the King.

## Ready to Start?

You have your gear. You have the playbook. The field is ready. It is time to start the search. We begin with the most important person in the universe. We begin with the one who started it all. Let's look at the God who was there before time began. He is your Creator, your King, and your Father.

*Psst: Don't forget to check out the Extra Content Sections at the end of this book!*

# SECTION ONE

## KNOW YOUR HOLY CREATOR

*Every team starts with a founder. Before the first whistle ever blew, someone had to build the stadium. Someone had to write the rulebook and pick the colors for the jerseys. In your life, that founder is God. This first part focuses on the Creator who started it all. You cannot know the purpose of the game if you do not know the one who created it. We start here because God is the foundation for everything else. He is the one who gives you breath to run and the strength to compete.*

*In these chapters, we will look at who God is. We will see that he has always been here and always will be. We will see how he talks to us through his own book. We will even look at the Father, Son, and Spirit. Finally, we will learn why we can trust him even when the score does not look good. Knowing God is the first step in your training. It gives you a reason to play with your whole heart. Get ready to meet the one who made the stars and the one who made you.*

# CHAPTER 1

## MEET THE GOD WHO LIVES FOREVER

You know that feeling when you step onto a fresh field? The grass is cut. The lines are painted. Everything looks ready. But have you ever stopped to think about who made the dirt under your cleats? Or who made the air you breathe while you sprint? We usually focus on the game right in front of us. We worry about the next play or the halftime score. But there is a much bigger story going on. It starts with a God who does not have a "start" button.

### He Has No Birthday

Everything you own has a beginning. Your favorite basketball came out of a box. Your bike was put together in a shop. Even you have a birthday that your family celebrates every year. But God is different. He is the only one who was never born. He never had a first day of school. He never had a "rookie season." He has simply always been.

The Bible uses a specific phrase for this. It says God is the "Alpha and the Omega." In the old Greek language, Alpha was the first letter of the alphabet and Omega was the last. It is like saying God is the A and the Z. He covers every single thing from the very start to the very end. He lives outside of time. While we measure our days by clocks and calendars, God just *is*.

### The Coach Who Never Quits

Think about the toughest coach you know. That coach might stay late at the gym or get up early to watch film. But eventually, even the best coach has to go home and sleep. They get tired. Their voices get scratchy. They grow old and eventually stop coaching.

God never gets tired. He never needs a nap. He does not drink coffee to stay awake. The Bible says that he never slumbers or sleeps.

This is a huge deal for you. It means that when you pray at three in the morning, he is listening. When you are nervous before a big 6:00 AM game, he is already awake and with you. His energy levels are always at 100 percent. He is the only one in the universe who does not need to recharge.

## He Is the "I AM"

One time, a man named Moses asked God what his name was. He wanted to know what to call the person who was talking to him from a burning bush. God didn't give him a long list of titles or a fancy nickname. He just said, "I AM WHO I AM."

That sounds a bit strange at first, right? But it is actually very cool. It means God does not depend on anyone else to exist. He doesn't need a battery. He doesn't need to eat food to stay alive. He is the source of all life. Everything else in the world, the trees, the dogs, the oceans, and your teammates, needs God to keep going. But God doesn't need anything. He is perfectly happy and strong all by himself.

## Seeing the Whole Field

In sports, we call it "vision." A great quarterback can see the whole field. They know where the defenders are and where their receivers are going. But even the best player can only see what is happening *right now*. They cannot see what will happen in the third quarter while they are still in the first.

God has perfect vision, but not just for space. He has perfect vision for time. He sees your past, your present, and your future all at once. He knows what the score will be before the game even starts. He knows where you will be ten years from now. Because he is eternal, he is already there. This should take a lot of pressure off your shoulders. You do not have to worry about the future because your Coach is already in the future waiting for you.

## Why This Matters on the Sidelines

Why do we need to know that God lives forever? Because it makes him a "Rock." If you try to build a house on sand, it will wash away when the rain hits. If you build your life on things that change, like how many points you score or how many friends you have, you will eventually feel let down. Friends move away. Stats go down. Trophies get dusty in the attic.

God never changes. He is the same yesterday, today, and forever. His love for you today is just as strong as it was when he made the world. It will be just as strong when you are ninety years old. When everything else in your life feels like it is shifting or moving, you can hold onto God. He is the only thing in the universe that is truly permanent.

## Join the Winning Team

Following an eternal God means you are on a team that can never truly lose. Even when things look bad on the scoreboard of life, we know how the story ends. God wins. He has already told us that he is the King of ages. He invites you to be part of his kingdom. This isn't a team that will fold or go out of business. It is a kingdom that lasts forever.

When you play for God, you are playing for a reward that never fades. Most athletes play for a plastic trophy or a cheap medal. Those are fun for a day, but they don't last. God offers you a life with him that goes on forever. That is the ultimate championship.

## The Never-Ending Story

Most books have a final page. Most seasons have a final game. But your life with God does not have a "Game Over" screen. Because he is eternal, he can give you eternal life. This doesn't just mean you live a long time. It means you get to know the most amazing person in the universe forever.

So, next time you are running a lap or sitting on the bench, remember the God who lives forever. He was there when the first mountain was formed. He is here right now while you are reading this. And he will be there in a million years. He is the Alpha and the Omega. He is your Creator, and he is ready for the next play.

## Your Daily Training

How do you act when you know God is eternal?

- **Be Patient:** If God isn't in a hurry, you don't have to be either. Trust his timing for your life.

- **Be Bold:** You are on the side of the King who never loses. You don't have to be afraid of what people think.
- **Be Thankful:** Every breath you take is a gift from the one who holds time in his hands.

God is not just a character from an old book. He is the living, breathing, eternal King. He wants you to know him today. Not just as a set of facts, but as your Coach and your Father. The race is long, but you aren't running it alone. The one who started the race is running right beside you.

# CHAPTER 2

## READ GOD'S OWN BOOK

Imagine you just joined a new sports team. You walk into the locker room and see a thick binder sitting on your bench. Your name is written on the front in big letters. Inside, you find everything you need to know to succeed. It has the plays for the next game. It has a list of the best foods to eat for energy. It even has a personal letter from the head coach explaining how much he believes in you. The Bible is like that binder, but it is much more important. It is the specific message that the Creator of the universe sent directly to you.

### God Speaks to Us

We cannot know what God thinks just by looking at the clouds or the trees. We can see that he is smart and strong by looking at nature. However, nature does not tell us how God feels about us. It does not tell us how he wants us to live. To know those things, God had to speak. He chose to use human language so we could understand him clearly.

The Bible is not just a book filled with good advice from smart people. It is the actual Word of God. The writers were real men like David, Moses, and Peter. They used their own styles and backgrounds to write. Yet, God guided their minds so perfectly that every word they wrote was exactly what he wanted to say. A famous verse in the Bible says that all scripture is breathed out by God. This means the words came from his own breath. When you read the Bible, you are listening to God talk.

### The Ultimate Scout Report

In sports, a scout report tells you the truth about your opponent and your own team. It helps you prepare for what is coming. The Bible acts as the ultimate scout report for your life. It tells you the truth about the world around you. It shows you where the traps are located. It also shows you the path to victory.

You can trust this report because God cannot lie. People make mistakes all the time. Scientists change their minds when they find new facts. Even your favorite sports analysts get their predictions wrong. God knows everything from the beginning to the end. His Word never needs an update. It is just as true today as it was thousands of years ago. You can build your whole life on these pages without worrying that the rules will change tomorrow.

## One Big Story

The Bible looks like one big book, but it is actually a collection of sixty-six smaller books. These were written over a period of about 1,500 years by about forty different people. Some were kings, while others were fishermen or shepherds. You might think a book like that would be a mess. If forty different people tried to write one story over a thousand years, it would usually be full of contradictions.

Instead, the Bible tells one perfectly linked story. From the first page to the last, it points to the same plan. It shows how God created us, how we turned away, and how he sent a Savior to bring us back. This unity is a miracle. It proves that there was one main Author behind all those different writers. God was the Master Coach directing every person to play their part in the narrative.

## Why You Need the Playbook

A playbook is useless if it stays in your bag during the game. You have to study it until you know the moves by heart. The same is true for the Bible. We read it so we can know God better. We do not read it just to win arguments or look smart in Sunday school. We read it to hear the voice of our Father.

The Bible is like a lamp that shows you where to step when the world feels dark. It gives you wisdom when you have to make a tough choice at school. It gives you comfort when you lose a big game or feel lonely. Most importantly, it tells you how to be saved. It is the only book in the world that can show you the way to eternal life.

## How to Use Your Equipment

You probably have a routine for your sport. You stretch, you warm up, and you practice your drills. You should have a routine for reading God's Word too. Try to read a small part of it every single day. Do not feel like you have to read ten chapters at once. Even a few verses can give you something to think about while you run your laps.

Ask God to help you understand what you are reading. Since he is the Author, he is the best person to explain it to you. Look for what the text says about God first. Ask yourself what it teaches you about his character. Then, look for how you can apply it to your own life. Are there any commands to obey? Are there any promises to trust?

## It Is More Than Ink and Paper

The Bible is a living book. This means it has the strength to change the way you think and act. It can reach into your heart and show you things about yourself that nobody else sees. Sometimes it might make you feel uncomfortable because it points out where you are going wrong. Other times it will fill you with more joy than a championship win.

Every time you open the Bible, you are meeting with the King. He wants to coach you through every situation you face. He wants to encourage you when you are tired. He wants to give you a goal that is bigger than any trophy. Do not let this book gather dust on your shelf. Pick it up and see what the Coach has to say to you today.

## Staying in the Game

There will be times when reading the Bible feels hard. You might find parts that are confusing or names that are difficult to say. Do not give up when that happens. Just like a hard workout, the effort is worth the result. The more you read, the more the pieces will start to fit together. You will start to see the beauty of God's plan in every chapter.

Your Bible is the most valuable piece of equipment you will ever own. It is a gift from a God who loves you enough to tell you the truth. Treat it with respect and study it with excitement. The words on these pages are the very words of life. They will keep you on the right track until you reach the finish line.

# CHAPTER 3

## LOOK AT THE FATHER, SON, AND SPIRIT

Getting to know God can feel like trying to understand a very deep team strategy. You see different people on the field doing various jobs, but they all belong to the same organization. The Bible shows us a special truth about God that we call the Trinity. While that specific word is not in the Bible, the idea shows up on almost every single page. We believe in one God who exists as three distinct persons. These are the Father, the Son, and the Holy Spirit.

### One Team and One God

The most important thing to keep in mind is that there is only one God. Christians do not worship three separate gods. That would be like saying a team has three different head coaches who never talk or agree. The Bible says clearly that the Lord is one. However, this one God is never lonely. He has always lived in a perfect relationship within himself.

Think about a triangle for a moment. A triangle is one single shape. Yet, it has three distinct corners. If you take away one corner, the triangle is gone. Each corner is part of the same one thing. This is a small way to picture how the Father, the Son, and the Spirit are all the same one God. They are equal in power and have lived forever.

### The Work of the Father

We often think of God the Father as the creator and the one who holds the big plan. He is the person who sent his Son into the world because his love for us is so huge. The Father provides what we need and listens when we pray. He acts like the owner of the team who provides the stadium, the uniforms, and the chance to play. He watches over everything with a kind and steady eye.

The Father is perfectly holy and fair. You can trust him to keep his word because he has the power to make things happen. He is the source of every good thing we enjoy. When we call him our Father, we are talking about a relationship where we are safe. We are cared for by the strongest person in the universe.

## The Work of the Son

Jesus Christ is the Son of God. He is not a separate god. He is the Word of God who became a human being. He came to earth to show us exactly what the Father is like. If you want to know how God feels about people who are hurting or lost, you just have to look at Jesus. He is the person of the Trinity who stepped onto the field to play the game for us.

Jesus lived a perfect life that we could never achieve on our own. He followed every rule in the Bible without making a single error. Then he took the penalty for our mistakes so we could join God's family. He is our Captain and our Savior. He is the hero who won the ultimate victory over death. Even though he is back in heaven now, he remains fully God and fully man.

## The Work of the Spirit

The Holy Spirit is often the person of the Trinity that kids find the most mysterious. He does not have a physical body like Jesus did, but he is just as much God as the Father and the Son. The Spirit is like the internal drive and wisdom that helps an athlete perform at their peak. He lives inside every person who follows Jesus.

The Holy Spirit helps us understand the Bible when we read it. He gives us the strength to say no to things that are wrong. He also comforts us when we feel sad or afraid. Think of him as the Coach who is always with you on the sidelines. He whispers the truth to your heart and reminds you of what Jesus taught. He is the one who changes us from the inside out so we can look more like our Captain every day.

## Working Together for You

The Father, the Son, and the Spirit always work together in perfect harmony. They never argue about what to do next. They never have different goals. When God created the world, all three persons were there. When Jesus was baptized in the river, the Father spoke from heaven and the Spirit came down like a dove. They are the perfect team.

This matters for your life because it shows that God is a God of love. Before anything else was made, the Father, Son, and Spirit loved each other. Because God is a relationship, he made you for a relationship too. He wants you to know the Father, follow the Son, and listen to the Spirit. You are invited to join in the life of God.

## Why This Knowledge Is a Huge Advantage

Knowing about the Trinity helps you see how big and amazing God really is. He is much more than just a powerful man in the sky. He is a beautiful being who is far beyond what we can imagine. This should make us feel a sense of wonder. We serve a King who is so great that we cannot even fully explain him with simple words.

When you are out on the field, remember that you are never alone. The Father is watching over you as your provider. The Son is leading you as your Captain. The Holy Spirit is inside you giving you the power to act with courage. You have the whole team of heaven on your side. That kind of support gives you a confidence that no opponent can ever shake.

## Training Your Heart

You might not understand everything about the Trinity today. That is perfectly fine. Even the smartest adults still find it hard to explain. The goal is not to solve a math puzzle but to know a person. Spend time talking to each person of the Trinity. Thank the Father for making you. Thank the Son for saving you. Ask the Holy Spirit to guide your steps at school and during your games.

As you grow, you will see the fingerprints of the Father, Son, and Spirit all over your life. You will see how they work together to lead you toward the finish line. You belong to a God who is one, yet three. He is your Creator, your Savior, and your Comforter. Stay close to him and watch how he uses his power to help you grow into the athlete and person he wants you to be.

# CHAPTER 4

## TRUST THE GOD WHO RULES EVERYTHING

Think about a game where the referee has lost total control of the field. Players are breaking rules left and right, the scoreboard is blinking random numbers, and nobody knows which way to run. It would be impossible to play your best in a mess like that. Thankfully, the universe is not a chaotic mess. God is in total control of every single thing that happens. We call this his sovereignty. It means he is the ultimate King who rules over the stars, the shifting weather, and even the final score of your game.

### The King on the Throne

God does not just watch the world go by like a fan sitting in the back of the bleachers. He is the one running the entire show from start to finish. He has the authority to do whatever he pleases, and his plans never fail. The Bible says that our God is in the heavens and he does all that he purposed. Not a single sparrow falls to the ground without him knowing about it. If he cares about the life of a tiny bird, you can be sure he cares about every small detail of your day.

This can be hard to wrap our minds around when things go wrong. We might wonder why God allows a rainout on the day of a big tournament or why he lets a teammate get injured. We have to remember that God sees the whole map while we only see the next turn in the road. He is like a master coach who sees the end of the long season from the very first day of summer practice. He uses even the tough times to build our character and lead us toward his good goals. He is never surprised by a bad bounce or a late goal.

## No Accidents in the Plan

Sometimes we use the word luck. We say someone got a lucky bounce or a lucky break at the buzzer. In reality, there is no such thing as luck when you follow the King of the universe. Every "bounce" in life is under his watch. This does not mean we should be lazy and stop practicing our drills. God wants us to work hard and give our best effort in everything we do. But we can rest at night knowing that the results are always in his hands.

Knowing that God rules everything takes the heavy pressure off your shoulders. You do not have to carry the weight of the whole world. You just have to be faithful to your part of the plan. If you win the championship, you can thank him for the victory. If you lose the game, you can trust that he has a reason for that outcome too. He is working all things together for the good of those who love him. He is the one who decides when the sun rises and when the rain falls.

## Freedom from the Weight of Worry

Worry is like trying to run laps while wearing a heavy backpack filled with rocks. It slows you down and makes you tired before the game even starts. Most of our worry comes from trying to control things we cannot change. We worry about what other people think or what might happen at school tomorrow. But when you realize that God is the one in charge, you can drop that backpack on the ground.

The Bible tells us not to be anxious about anything. We can trade our worry for prayer because we know the King is our Father. He has the power to provide for you and the wisdom to lead you through the dark. Since he is already in control of tomorrow, you can focus on doing your best today. You are safe in the hands of the one who commands the wind and the waves with a single word. He is never overwhelmed by the problems we face.

## Trusting the Process of Training

In sports, you have to trust the process. You might not see why a coach makes you do a certain boring drill until months later when you are in the middle of a game. Trusting God is very similar to that. His ways are much higher than our ways. We might think we know the best path to take, but he knows the perfect path that leads to growth.

There will be days when the "play" God has called for your life does not make sense to you. Those are the moments when your trust is tested. Remind yourself of who is in charge of the universe. He is the God who lives forever. He is the God who wrote the Book you read. He is the Father, the Son, and the Holy Spirit. Because he is all of those things, he is worthy of your total trust even when the score looks bad.

## A Peace That Stays with You

When you truly believe that God rules everything, you gain a special kind of peace. It is a quiet confidence that stays with you even when the stadium is loud or the pressure is high. This peace does not come from your own skills or your own strength. It comes from knowing that your King is sitting on his throne and he loves you.

This does not mean life will always be easy or that you will win every trophy. It means that even when life is hard, you are never alone on the field. Your Coach is not surprised by the challenges you face. He is using every circumstance to make you stronger and to show his glory to the world. Stand firm in that truth. The God who rules the vast universe is the same God who calls you his own child. He has the final say in all things, and his kingdom will never end.

## Resting in His Power

At the end of a long day, you can lay your head down and sleep because God is awake. He does not need to rest, so you can. You do not have to stay up wondering if the world will fall apart. He is holding the stars in place and keeping your heart beating. His sovereignty is like a soft pillow for a tired athlete.

When you wake up, remember that you are walking into a day that God has already planned. Whether you face a big test, a hard practice, or a fun day with friends, he is in charge. He has given you exactly what you need for the tasks ahead. Trust his power, rely on his wisdom, and play your heart out for the King who rules everything.

# SECTION TWO

## FOLLOW THE LIVING SAVIOR

*Every team needs that one star player who can step up and change the whole game. You know the type. When the score is down, the crowd is quiet, and the clock is ticking toward zero, you look for the person who can carry the weight of the team. In the history of the whole world, that person is Jesus Christ. This second part is all about the Savior who stepped out of heaven and onto our messy field. We call him the living Savior because he is not just a name in an old history book or a statue in a building. He is alive right now.*

*In the next four chapters, we are going to follow the path of Jesus from his humble start in a barn to his massive victory over the grave. We will see why he is the hero the world was waiting for since the very beginning. We will watch how he played the game of life without breaking a single rule. Then, we will look at the most important moment in all of history: his sacrifice on the cross and his return to life. Understanding Jesus is the key to understanding everything else in your life. He is the Captain of our faith and the only one who can lead us across the finish line.*

# CHAPTER 1

## SEE THE PROMISED HERO ARRIVE

If you have ever sat by your phone waiting for a massive trade or a new superstar to join your team, you know that waiting is the hardest part. You check the news every five minutes. You imagine how much the team will change once the big name finally shows up. For thousands of years, the people in the Bible were stuck in that same waiting room. They were looking for a Hero. God promised a Savior right after the very first sin happened in the garden. He told his people that a King was coming to crush the power of evil and set them free for good.

### A Very Strange Entrance

When a famous athlete arrives in a new city, you usually see flashing lights and expensive cars. You see big crowds and fancy hotels. But when the King of the entire universe arrived on earth, he did not come with a parade. He did not check into a mansion or move into a palace. Instead, Jesus was born in a quiet, dusty town called Bethlehem. His first bed was a manger. That is just a wooden box where people put hay for cows and sheep to eat.

This tells you something huge about your Hero. Jesus did not come to show off or act like he was too good for us. He came to be near us. He became a real human being with skin and bones. He felt the cold. He got hungry. He had to learn how to walk just like you did. The Bible calls him Immanuel. That name means "God with us." He stepped off his throne and entered our world to play on our level.

### Checking the Scouting Reports

Long before Jesus took his first breath, God gave his people scouting reports called prophecies. These were specific clues written down by prophets hundreds of years before the birth of Christ. They told the people exactly where the Savior would be born and what his family tree would look like.

- The reports said he would be born in the small town of Bethlehem.
- They said he would come from the royal family of King David.
- They said his mother would be a virgin.

Jesus hit every single one of those marks. The odds of one person doing that by accident are impossible. It would be like a player predicting every single play of a game perfectly before it even started. This proves that Jesus was not just a lucky teacher. He was the one God planned to send since the world began. He was the promised Hero, and he showed up right on time.

## Both God and Man

This is the most amazing part of the whole playbook. Jesus is 100 percent God and 100 percent man at the same time. It is a mystery that is hard to explain, but it is why he is the only one who can save us. Because he is a man, he can represent you. He knows what it feels like to be tempted or to feel sad. He knows what it is like to have sore muscles after a long day of work.

Because he is God, he has the power to fix what is broken. He has the authority to forgive every bad choice you have ever made. He has the strength to defeat death itself. Think of it like a coach who was once a world-class player. He knows the struggle because he played the game, but he has the master plan to lead the team to a win. Jesus is the bridge between heaven and earth.

## The Mission of the Hero

Why did the Hero come? He did not show up just to do cool miracles or give long speeches. He came on a rescue mission. The world was stuck on a losing streak because of sin. We were separated from God and could not find the way back home on our own. Jesus arrived to be our substitute. He came to live the life we should have lived and to take the penalty we deserved.

His arrival was the start of the greatest comeback story in history. From the moment he breathed in the air of that stable, he was heading toward a goal. He was focused on the work of his Father. He was here to win back what was lost and to invite you onto his winning team. The Hero has arrived, and the world will never be the same again.

# CHAPTER 2

## WATCH JESUS LIVE A PERFECT LIFE

Imagine a player who goes through an entire career without ever making a single mistake. This player never misses a shot, never drops a pass, and never commits a foul. In the world of sports, that is basically impossible. Even the greatest legends have bad days or make poor choices when the pressure is high. But when Jesus stepped onto the earth, he did something no one else has ever done. He lived a life of total perfection. He followed every single rule of God with a perfect heart and perfect actions every single second of his life.

### The Training Ground of Nazareth

Jesus did not start his public work until he was about thirty years old. Before he was a famous teacher, he was a child and a young man living in a humble town called Nazareth. He grew up in a regular home and worked with his hands as a carpenter. This part of his life is very important for us to see. It shows that he understands what it is like to be a kid and a teenager. He knows what it feels like to have chores to do and lessons to learn.

The Bible tells us that Jesus grew in wisdom and in stature. He also grew in favor with God and man. He had to learn his lessons at school and obey his parents at home. Even as a boy, he was focused on his Father's business. He lived a quiet life of obedience, preparing for the big mission ahead. He was training in the small things so that he would be ready for the big things. Think of this as the long years of practice that nobody sees before the championship game. Jesus was faithful in the workshop and in the home long before he was famous.

## Facing the Ultimate Opponent

Before Jesus started his ministry, he went into the wilderness for forty days. While he was there, he was tempted by the devil. This was like a championship match between good and evil with the highest stakes imaginable. The devil tried to get Jesus to cheat, to show off, and to take the easy way out. He used every trick in the book to try and make Jesus stumble or doubt who he was.

Jesus did not give in for even a second. Every time the devil tempted him, Jesus fought back with the Word of God. He quoted scripture to keep his mind focused on the truth. Because he stayed strong, he proved that he was the perfect Hero. He succeeded where everyone else had failed. He showed that he had the discipline and the power to overcome any temptation that comes our way. When you feel tempted to cheat or quit, remember that your Captain has already beaten that opponent.

## Playing for the Father's Glory

When Jesus began traveling and teaching, people were amazed by him. He healed the sick, made the blind see, and even walked on water during a storm. He had all the power in the world, yet he never once used it for himself. He did not try to become a rich king or a famous celebrity. Every miracle he performed was done to show people who God is and to help those who were hurting.

Jesus always did exactly what the Father told him to do. He said that his food was to do the will of the one who sent him. He lived with a single goal: to honor God. Whether he was talking to a huge crowd on a mountain or sitting quietly with a friend, his heart was always in the right place. He loved people perfectly, even when they were mean to him. He spoke the truth perfectly, even when it was hard to hear. He was never "faking it" for the cameras. He was the real deal.

## Our Perfect Representative

Why did Jesus have to be perfect? Why couldn't he just be a "mostly good" person like us? The answer is found in the rules of the game. God is perfectly holy, and we are not. Because of our sin, we are disqualified from being in God's presence. We needed someone to play the game in our place. We needed a substitute who could turn in a perfect scorecard.

Jesus lived that life for you. When God looks at those who follow Jesus, he does not see our mistakes and our fouls. He sees the perfect record of his Son. Jesus earned the "win" that we could never earn on our own. He is like a captain who scores all the points for a team that was losing. Because he was perfect, he was the only one who could eventually pay the price for our sins. If he had sinned even once, he could not have saved us.

## Learning from the Master

Watching Jesus live his life gives us the best example of how we should live. He showed us how to be brave when people are being bullies. He showed us how to be kind to people that everyone else ignores. He showed us that true greatness comes from serving others rather than trying to be the most important person in the room. He washed the feet of his disciples, showing that no job is too small for a leader.

When you are at school or on the field, you can ask yourself how Jesus would handle the situation. How would he treat a teammate who made a mistake? How would he act when a referee makes a bad call? While we will never be perfect like he is, we can move in the right direction by following his lead. We have the best Coach in history showing us the way. He does not just tell us what to do; he showed us how to do it.

## A Life of Constant Prayer

One of the most interesting things about the perfect life of Jesus was how much he prayed. Even though he was God, he spent hours talking to his Father. He would often get up very early in the morning or go up on a mountain alone to pray. This was the secret to his strength. He stayed connected to the source of his power every single day.

This teaches us that even the strongest person needs to rely on God. If Jesus needed to pray to live a godly life, how much more do we need to pray? He shows us that a perfect life is a life of dependence. It is not about being "tough" enough to do it alone. It is about staying close to the Father and listening to his voice. Prayer was the "huddle" where Jesus got his instructions.

## The Finish Line in Sight

Jesus lived every day knowing that a very difficult day was coming. He knew his perfect life would eventually lead him to the cross. He did not run away from that destiny or try to hide. He stayed the course with courage and love. His perfection was not just for show; it was part of the rescue plan. He was the perfect Lamb of God who was preparing to give his life for his friends.

As you follow Jesus through the pages of the Bible, pay attention to the small details. Notice his kindness to children, his honesty with leaders, and his total obedience to his Father. There has never been anyone like him, and there never will be again. He is the living Savior who lived the perfect life so that we could have a renewed life in him. His victory is now our victory.

## Consistency Under Pressure

Think about the times you have felt the most pressure. Maybe it was a final exam or the last minute of a tie game. It is easy to be "good" when things are easy, but it is hard when things get tough. Jesus was perfect even when people were shouting at him and trying to trap him. He never lost his temper in a sinful way. He never lied to protect himself.

His consistency is what makes him so trustworthy. You never have to wonder which "version" of Jesus you are going to get. He is the same yesterday, today, and forever. His perfect life is a solid rock you can stand on when your own life feels shaky. When you feel like a failure, you can look at his success and remember that he is on your team.

## The Power of His Words

Jesus did not just act perfectly; he spoke perfectly too. He said things that changed the world forever. He taught us to love our enemies and to pray for those who treat us badly. He told stories that helped us understand God's love in a new way. Even the people who didn't like him had to admit that nobody ever spoke like he did.

Every word that came out of his mouth was filled with truth and grace. He never used his words to tear people down just to make himself look big. He used his words to heal, to teach, and to lead. This is another area where we can watch him and learn. If we want to be like our Captain, we need to watch how we speak to our teammates, our teachers, and our families.

## Final Thoughts on a Perfect Life

The perfect life of Jesus is the foundation of our faith. Without it, we would have no hope of being right with God. He did the hard work of obeying every command so that we could enjoy the blessing of being called God's children. It is a gift we could never buy and a trophy we could never win on our own.

As you go through your week, try to keep your eyes on the Master. Study his moves in the Bible. Listen to his coaching through the Holy Spirit. Remember that you are following the only person who ever played the game perfectly. He is not just a model to follow; he is the Savior who holds you up when you fall.

# CHAPTER 3

## STAND NEAR THE CROSS

In every great sports movie, there is a moment where it looks like the hero has lost. The star player is down on the turf, the lights are dimming, and the opposing team is celebrating. To anyone watching, the game is over. Standing near the cross of Jesus feels like that moment. It is the darkest part of the story. If you were there that day, you would have seen a crowd mocking a man who was dying. You would have seen his friends running away in fear. It looked like a total defeat. But in reality, this was the most important victory in the history of the universe. This was the moment the "Promised Hero" finished his biggest mission.

### The Most Difficult Play

We have talked about how Jesus lived a perfect life. He never committed a foul. He never broke a rule. Because of that, he was the only person who did not deserve to die. Death is the penalty for sin, and since Jesus had no sin, death had no claim on him. Yet, he chose to go to the cross anyway. He did not go because he was caught or because he was weak. He went because it was the only way to save us.

Think of it like a teammate taking a massive hit so that you can score the winning goal. Jesus took the "hit" for every bad thing we have ever done. All of our lies, our anger, and our selfishness were placed on his shoulders. The Bible says that he became sin for us. While he hung on that cross, he was paying a debt that he did not owe because we owed a debt we could never pay. It was the most difficult "play" ever called, and Jesus ran it perfectly.

## The Weight of the World

When Jesus was in the garden the night before he died, he was in deep agony. He knew what was coming. He wasn't just afraid of the physical pain, although the cross was a terrible way to die. He was feeling the weight of the Father's justice against sin. Throughout his whole life, Jesus had been in perfect, happy fellowship with God the Father. On the cross, that was going to change.

As Jesus hung there, the sky went pitch black in the middle of the afternoon. It was as if the sun refused to watch. Jesus cried out, asking why God had forsaken him. In that moment, he was experiencing the separation from God that we deserved. He was being shut out so that we could be let in. He was treated like an enemy so that we could be treated like friends. He carried the weight of the world's darkness so we could walk in the light.

## The Words from the Cross

Even while he was in terrible pain, Jesus was still coaching us on how to love. He didn't scream threats at the people who were hurting him. Instead, he prayed for them. He asked the Father to forgive them because they didn't understand what they were doing. He also made sure his mother was cared for, showing that he never stopped being a loving son.

One of the men being executed next to Jesus realized who he was. This man was a criminal who had actually done wrong things. He asked Jesus to remember him. Jesus didn't tell him it was too late or that he needed to go back and do good deeds first. He told the man, "Today you will be with me in paradise." This shows us that the cross is for everyone. It doesn't matter how many games you have lost or how many mistakes you have made. If you turn to Jesus, his victory becomes yours.

## "It Is Finished"

Right before Jesus died, he shouted out three powerful words: "It is finished!" In the original language, this was a word used by businessmen when a bill was paid in full. It was also a word a general might use when a war was won. Jesus wasn't saying, "I am finished," like a person who has given up. He was saying that the work of salvation was complete.

The "score" was settled. The sacrifice was made. There was nothing left for us to do to earn our way to God. The bridge that had been broken back in the Garden of Eden was now fixed. When Jesus died, a thick curtain in the Temple tore in half from top to bottom. This was God's way of showing that the door was wide open. Anyone could now come to him through Jesus. The game-winning play had been executed, and the clock hit zero on the power of sin.

## Why the Blood Matters

You might wonder why there had to be so much pain and blood. Why couldn't God just say, "I forgive you," and leave it at that? The reason is that God is perfectly just. If a judge let a criminal go free without any punishment, that judge wouldn't be a good judge. Someone had to pay the price for the rules we broke.

The blood of Jesus is what cleans us. Just like you might use water to wash the mud off your jersey after a rainy game, the blood of Jesus washes the stain of sin off our souls. Because he was the perfect Son of God, his sacrifice was big enough to cover every person who has ever lived. He was the "Lamb of God" who took away the sin of the world. It was a high price, but he paid it because he saw you were worth it.

## Standing in the Shadow of the Cross

When we stand near the cross in our minds, we see two things at the same time. We see how bad our sin is, and we see how great God's love is. Our sin must be very serious if it took the death of the Son of God to fix it. But God's love must be incredibly deep if he was willing to go through that for us.

For an athlete, the cross is the ultimate lesson in sacrifice. It shows us that true strength isn't about crushing others; it's about giving yourself for others. Jesus didn't use his power to save himself; he used his power to stay on that cross until the job was done. He showed us that the way to lead is to serve. When you feel like you have to be the best and the most famous to be important, look at the cross. The King of the world made himself nothing so that you could have everything.

## The Silence of the Saturday

After Jesus died, his friends took his body down and put it in a tomb. They rolled a massive stone in front of the entrance. It was a very sad and quiet time. His followers thought they had lost. They didn't understand yet that the "defeat" of the cross was actually the secret to their victory.

Sometimes in our lives, it feels like "Saturday." It feels like God is silent and the bad guys are winning. We might feel like our prayers aren't being heard or that our mistakes are too big to fix. But we have to remember that Friday's cross happened for a reason, and Sunday is coming. The cross wasn't an accident. It was the plan. God was working even when it looked like he was losing.

## A Love That Never Quits

If you ever doubt if God loves you, you only have to look at the cross. You don't have to wonder if he cares or if he is listening. He proved his love in the most dramatic way possible. He didn't just say "I love you" from a distance; he came down and bled for you. He went through the worst pain imaginable so that he would never have to be without you.

This changes the way we live. We don't follow God because we are afraid of getting in trouble. We follow him because we are amazed by what he did on that hill. We play our best because we want to honor the Captain who gave his life for the team. The cross is the place where we find our true identity. We are people who were worth dying for.

## Training Your Heart at the Cross

How does standing near the cross change your daily life at school or on the team?

- **It kills pride:** You can't brag about how good you are when you realize you needed a Savior to die for you.

- **It gives courage:** If Jesus died for you, you don't have to be afraid of what people think of you.

- **It teaches forgiveness:** If God forgave you for so much, you can forgive your teammate who messed up.

The cross is the center of everything we believe. It is the moment where the Hero took our place and won the war. It looks like a tragedy, but it is actually the greatest victory ever. Take a moment to thank Jesus for staying on that cross. He did it for his Father's glory, and he did it for you.

# CHAPTER 4

## CELEBRATE THE KING WHO ROSE AGAIN

Think about the biggest comeback you have ever seen. Maybe your team was down by twenty points with only a few minutes left on the clock. The fans were already heading for the parking lot. The other side was laughing on the sidelines, basically celebrating a win that hadn't happened yet. It looked like the lights were about to go out on your season. Then, everything flipped. A quick score, a big defensive stop, and suddenly the momentum shifted so fast it made your head spin. You won a game that nobody thought was possible.

The resurrection of Jesus is the ultimate version of that story. It is the greatest comeback in the history of the world. It is the moment where the "losing side" walked off the field as the undisputed champions of the universe.

### The Sunday Morning Surprise

On the Sunday morning after Jesus died on the cross, a few of his friends walked toward his tomb. They weren't carrying pom-poms or victory signs. They were carrying heavy spices to put on a dead body. They weren't expecting a miracle; they were expecting a funeral. They were sad, tired, and probably feeling like the last three years had been a massive waste of time. But when they rounded the corner into the garden, they saw something that stopped their hearts. The massive stone that sealed the grave had been tossed aside like a piece of trash.

An angel was sitting right there, and he didn't look like he was at a funeral. He gave them the news that changed every single thing about our world: "He is not here, for he has risen." That one sentence meant the grave couldn't hold him. It meant the "Game Over" screen was a lie. Jesus didn't just survive an injury. He conquered death itself. He walked out of that dark hole on his own two feet, breathing the morning air as the Champion of life.

## He Is Not a Ghost

Some people try to say the resurrection was just a nice dream or a vision. But the Bible goes out of its way to show that Jesus was physically, tangibly alive. He didn't just haunt a room like a blurry ghost. He met with his friends for breakfast. He walked on the dirt roads with them. He even ate a piece of fish to prove his stomach worked. One of his followers, a guy named Thomas, wouldn't believe it until he actually touched the scars on the hands of Jesus. Jesus let him do it. He wanted his team to have 100 percent proof that their Captain was back.

At one point, more than five hundred people saw him at the same time. This wasn't a secret. It was a public victory lap. Think about how many cameras and witnesses it takes to make a world record "official." Jesus had hundreds of witnesses who saw him, talked to him, and touched him. These people were so sure he was alive that they spent the rest of their lives telling the story, even when it got them thrown in jail. You don't die for a fairy tale. You die for a King you have seen with your own eyes.

## Breaking Death's Winning Streak

Why does a story from two thousand years ago matter to you today? It matters because death is the one opponent that scares everyone. Even the fastest athletes, the most powerful kings, and the smartest scientists eventually have to face the end. It is the ultimate "undefeated" rival. But when Jesus rose again, he broke death's winning streak for good. He proved that he has the keys to the grave in his pocket.

Because Jesus is alive, you don't have to live in fear. You know that this life on earth is just the pre-game. For everyone on Jesus' team, death is just a tunnel that leads to a much better stadium. It is a doorway to an eternal kingdom where there are no more injuries, no more losses, and no more pain. Jesus showed us the way through. He is the first one out of the grave, and he promises that we are going to follow him.

## The Receipt for the Cross

Remember how we talked about Jesus paying for our sins on the cross? The resurrection is like the receipt for that payment. If Jesus had stayed in the grave, we would never know for sure if his sacrifice actually worked. We might wonder if God the Father actually accepted the payment. But by raising Jesus from the dead, God was putting his official stamp of approval on the whole mission.

It was God's way of saying, "The price is paid. The work is finished. The win is in the books." The resurrection proves that Jesus is exactly who he said he was. He is the Son of God and the King of kings. If he has the power to bring himself back to life, he definitely has the power to handle your life. He can handle your biggest mistakes, your deepest fears, and your entire future.

## New Power for Your Daily Game

The resurrection didn't just happen so Jesus could be famous. It happened so you could have a new kind of power. The same strength that raised Jesus from the dead is now available to you through the Holy Spirit. This isn't just "positive thinking" or trying to be a better person on your own. It is real, spiritual energy that helps you live for God when things get tough.

Think about a controller for a video game. If the batteries are dead, it doesn't matter how hard you mash the buttons; the character on the screen won't move. But when you put in fresh batteries, it works perfectly. Before we know Jesus, we are like those dead batteries. We don't have the "juice" to live the way we were made to live. But because Jesus is alive, he plugs us into his own life. He gives us the strength to be kind when we want to be mean, and to be brave when we want to quit. We are living on resurrection power.

## You Serve a Living King

Most famous people from history are dead and gone. You can visit their graves or read their old books, but you can't have a conversation with them. You can't ask a coach from a hundred years ago for advice on your next play. But Jesus is a living King. You can talk to him right now. He is active in the world, and he is active in your life today.

This changes the way we worship. We don't just sing songs about a hero from the past. We sing to a Friend who is actually in the room. We don't just follow a list of old rules. We follow a Leader who is calling our name. Every time you step onto the field or into a classroom, you can know that the Living King is right there with you. You are playing for an audience of One, and he is more alive than anyone else in the stands.

## The Celebration That Never Ends

The resurrection is a reason to celebrate every single morning. In the early church, the followers of Jesus were so hyped about the resurrection that they moved their main meeting day to Sunday. They wanted to start every week remembering that their Captain won the war. That is why most churches meet on Sunday today. It is a weekly reminder that the tomb is empty and the King is on the throne.

As an athlete, this gives you a perspective that nobody can shake. If the worst thing that can happen to you is death, and Jesus has already beaten death, then what is there to really be afraid of? You can play with total freedom. You don't have to be perfect to be loved, because Jesus' victory is already credited to you. You can take risks, you can be humble, and you can give your all, knowing that the ultimate prize is already locked in.

## Training for a New Kind of Victory

How do you live like a "resurrection person" during the week?

- **Live with Hope:** Even when you have a bad day or a tough loss, remember that the story isn't over yet. God is the expert at comebacks.

- **Talk to the King:** Since he is alive, treat him like he is real. Share your worries and your big wins with him in prayer.

- **Share the News:** Tell your teammates the good news. You have a Savior who is more powerful than a stone grave!

The resurrection is the final piece of the puzzle. Without it, the cross is just a tragedy. With it, the cross is a total victory. Jesus Christ is not just a memory; he is the Master of the universe. He has finished the work, he has won the game, and he is inviting you to share in his glory.

Pick up your gear, head out to the field, and play with the joy of a champion. The tomb is empty, and the best is yet to come.

# SECTION THREE

## FACE THE PROBLEM OF SIN

*Every legendary story has a massive conflict. To truly value the victory Jesus won, we have to look closely at why we needed a rescue mission in the first place. This third part dives into the "injury" that affected the entire human race. We call it sin. It is the core reason the world feels broken and why we often struggle to do what is right, even when we want to.*

*In these four chapters, we are going back to the very start of the timeline. We will see the perfect world God designed and how things went off the tracks. We will look at why sin is such a big deal and why we cannot simply practice our way out of the problem. Understanding the weight of sin is not meant to make you feel bad. It is meant to show you how much you are loved. Once you realize how deep the hole was, you will see how amazing it is that God reached all the way down to pull you out.*

# CHAPTER 1

## START WITH A PERFECT CREATION

Before you can understand a broken bone on an X-ray, you have to know what a healthy bone looks like. To understand why the world is so messy today, we have to look back at the original blueprints. God did not create a world full of sadness, sickness, or mean teammates. In the beginning, everything was "very good." It was the ultimate home court, designed by the greatest Architect to be a place of total joy and peace.

### The Masterpiece of the Universe

God did not just throw the world together like a last-minute school project. He crafted it with incredible detail and care. He spoke, and light appeared out of nothing. He carved out the deep canyons and poured the massive oceans into place. He designed every leaf, every star, and every atom. When he got to the very end of his work, he created his most important masterpiece: human beings.

The Bible says that God made us in his own image. This does not mean we look like him physically, but that we were made to reflect his character to the rest of creation. We were made to be smart, creative, and loving. Most importantly, we were made to be in a close, walking relationship with him. Imagine being on a team where the Owner is your best friend and the Head Coach is your biggest fan. That was life in the Garden of Eden. There was no fear, no shame, and no hiding.

### No Fouls and No Errors

In this original world, there was no such thing as a "bad day." Adam and Eve, the first humans, lived in a place of perfect harmony. They didn't argue with each other or get their feelings hurt. They didn't feel lonely or anxious about the future. There were no injuries to worry about and no trophies to fight over because they already had everything they needed.

They had a job to do, which was to take care of the beautiful world God made. Work wasn't a tiring chore back then; it was a way to worship. They walked and talked with God in the cool of the day. There was no wall between heaven and earth. It was a world where every single play was successful and every moment was filled with purpose. You could say they were playing the game of life at the highest possible level, and they were winning every single day.

## The One Specific Rule

Even though they had total freedom to enjoy the garden, God gave them one specific boundary. He told them they could eat from any tree in the garden except for one: the Tree of the Knowledge of Good and Evil. This wasn't because God was being mean or trying to hide something fun from them. It was a test of trust and loyalty.

Every real relationship needs trust and the power to choose. For Adam and Eve to truly love God, they had to have the choice to follow him or walk away. The rule was there to remind them that God was the King and they were his people. As long as they stayed within that boundary, life would stay perfect. It was a simple rule for a perfect life. It gave them the chance to show God that they valued his wisdom more than their own desires.

## A Reflection of True Greatness

When you look at a beautiful sunset or see a perfectly executed play on the field, you are seeing a small "glimmer" of that original world. Deep down, we all feel like the world should be better than it is. We feel like things are "wrong" when we see people hurting or being unfair. That feeling exists because we were made for perfection. We were made for the Garden of Eden.

God's original plan shows us how much value we actually have. You aren't an accident or a random mistake. You aren't just a number on a jersey or a name on a roster. You are a high-definition image-bearer of the Living God. You were designed for greatness, for goodness, and for a friendship with your Creator that lasts forever. Starting with a perfect creation helps us see exactly what we lost when sin entered the picture. It also shows us exactly what Jesus came to win back for us in the end.

## The Purpose of the Design

Everything in a sports stadium has a purpose. The lights are there so you can see. The lines are there to define the field. The whistle is there to start the action. In the same way, everything in the original creation had a reason for existing. Humans were designed to be the "captains" of the earth, leading the way in showing how great God is.

When things work according to their design, they are beautiful. When a car stays on the road, it gets you where you need to go. When an athlete follows the play, the team succeeds. Adam and Eve were perfectly "on track" with God's design. They were living in the light, and there was no shadow of doubt or sin to be found. Understanding this perfection is the only way to realize how tragic the next part of the story really is.

## A World Without Shadows

In the Garden, there was no such thing as a secret. Adam and Eve were completely open with God and with each other. They didn't have to pretend to be someone else to be liked. They didn't have to perform to feel important. Their value didn't come from how fast they could run or how much they knew. It came from the fact that God made them and loved them.

This is the "gold standard" of life. It is the life we all go looking for when we try to be successful or popular. We are trying to get back to that feeling of being totally accepted and totally at peace. God started us off with that gift. He gave us a perfect start to the game. But as we will see in the next chapter, a new challenger was waiting in the shadows to try and ruin the perfect season.

# CHAPTER 2

## LEARN HOW SIN ENTERED THE WORLD

Every team has an opponent who plays dirty. You know the type. They wait for you to get tired, then they whisper things to get in your head. They try to make you doubt your coach or your own skills. In the perfect garden God made, an enemy showed up to do exactly that. He didn't use a physical weapon to ruin the world. He used a lie. This is the moment where the "perfect season" came to a crashing halt. It is the moment sin entered the game.

### The Great Deception

The Bible introduces a character called the serpent. He was clever and sneaky. He didn't walk up to Adam and Eve and tell them to hate God. Instead, he asked a very tricky question: "Did God actually say you shall not eat of any tree in the garden?" He wanted them to focus on the one thing they couldn't have instead of the thousands of things they could.

He made it sound like God was holding out on them. He suggested that God was keeping them back from something better. The serpent told them that if they ate the fruit, they would be like God. He made them believe that they didn't need a Coach anymore. He convinced them that they could be their own bosses and make their own rules. This was the first "foul" in human history, and it changed everything.

### The Choice That Broke the World

Adam and Eve listened to the lie. They looked at the fruit, they wanted it, and they took a bite. In that one moment, they stepped outside of the boundaries God had set. This was the birth of sin. Sin is not just "doing a bad thing." At its core, sin is a rebellion. It is telling God, "I know better than you do." It is like a player deciding to ignore every play the coach calls and just doing whatever they feel like on the field.

The second they ate the fruit, the world changed. The "perfect health" of creation vanished. Suddenly, they felt something they had never felt before: shame. They realized they were naked and they tried to hide from God among the trees. The friendship was broken. The light was gone. They had traded a relationship with the King for a piece of fruit, and the trade was a disaster.

## The Ripple Effect

When a key player on a team gets a serious injury, it doesn't just hurt them. It affects the whole roster. It changes the way the game is played for everyone. When Adam and Eve sinned, it caused a "spiritual injury" that passed down to every human being who would ever be born. It was like a virus that got into the DNA of the human race.

Because of that one choice, everything in creation started to wear out. This is why we have sickness, why plants grow thorns, and why we have to work so hard for everything we get. The harmony was gone. Animals started to fight, and people started to argue. Sin didn't just stay in that one garden. it spread like a shadow across the entire globe. Every mistake, every war, and every tear can be traced back to this moment in the locker room of history.

## The Blame Game

When God came looking for Adam and Eve, they didn't own up to what they did. Adam blamed Eve. Eve blamed the serpent. This was the very first "blame game." Instead of asking for forgiveness, they tried to point the finger at someone else. This is something we still do today. When we mess up a play or get a bad grade, our first instinct is often to blame the ref, the teacher, or our teammates.

Sin makes us want to hide the truth. It makes us want to look good on the outside even when things are messy on the inside. God saw right through their excuses. He is a holy God, and he cannot just ignore a broken rule. There had to be consequences for what happened. The perfect garden was no longer their home. They had to leave, and a massive angel was placed at the gate to keep them out. The "home court advantage" was officially lost.

## The First Promise of a Comeback

The story of how sin entered the world is very sad, but it ends with a glimmer of hope. Even while God was explaining the consequences of their sin, he made a promise. He told the serpent that one day, a son would be born to a woman who would crush the serpent's head. God was already planning the comeback.

He knew that Adam and Eve could never fix the problem on their own. They couldn't "practice" hard enough to get back into the garden. They needed a Hero to come and win the game for them. This was the first time the Gospel, the Good News, was ever mentioned. Even in the middle of their biggest failure, God was showing them that he still loved them. He provided clothes for them and promised a way back, even though it would take a long time and a massive sacrifice.

## Understanding the Opponent

To play a good game, you have to understand your opponent's tactics. The devil still uses the same tricks today that he used in the garden. He wants you to think that God's rules are meant to stop your fun. He wants you to believe that you can be your own king. He wants you to doubt that God really loves you.

When you feel those thoughts creeping in, remember Chapter 2. Remember that the serpent is a liar. God's boundaries are there to protect the "very good" life he designed for you. Sin always promises something great but leaves you hiding in the bushes, feeling ashamed. By learning how sin started, we can see why we need to stay close to our Coach. We can see that the only way to win is to trust the one who made the rules in the first place.

# CHAPTER 3

## SEE WHY PEOPLE NEED HELP

Think about a player who gets a serious injury during a game, like a torn ACL or a broken leg. No matter how much heart that player has, they cannot just "will" themselves to be healed. They cannot run a lap to fix a snapped bone. They need a surgeon. They need someone from the outside with the right tools to step in and repair what is broken. When sin entered the world, it wasn't just a small scratch or a minor penalty. It was a total system failure. The human race became "injured" in a way that we simply cannot fix by ourselves.

### The Problem of a Broken Nature

Because of what happened in the garden, every person is now born with a natural pull toward doing things their own way instead of God's way. You might have noticed that nobody has to teach a toddler how to be selfish or how to scream "Mine!" when they want a toy. We don't have to take classes to learn how to lie or how to get jealous of a teammate who gets more playing time. Those things come naturally to us because our internal "compass" is broken.

The Bible uses a heavy word for this: dead. It says that without God's help, we are spiritually dead in our sins. A dead person cannot help themselves. A person at the bottom of a deep well without a ladder cannot just jump out, no matter how much they practice their vertical leap. This is why we need help. We aren't just good people who occasionally make mistakes; we are people with a deep heart problem that we cannot solve on our own.

### The Trap of Being "Good Enough"

One of the biggest mistakes athletes make is thinking they can earn their way into God's favor by being better than the person next to them. We look at the "bad kids" or people who do terrible things and think, "Well, I'm doing okay. I follow the rules, I work hard, and I'm nice to my parents." We try to use our good deeds to balance out our bad ones, like trying to fix a failing grade by doing one extra credit assignment.

The problem is that God's standard isn't "better than average." His standard is 100 percent perfection. Imagine a basketball game where you have to make every single shot you take for your entire career, or you lose. One miss, and the game is over. That is what God's holiness requires. Even our very best days are still stained by selfish thoughts or pride. The Bible says our "righteous acts" are like filthy rags compared to God's purity. When we see how high the bar is, we realize that we are all stuck far below it.

## Why We Can't Coach Ourselves Out

In sports, a good coach can help you fix your form or improve your speed. But a coach cannot change your heart. You can follow all the drills and learn all the plays, but if you still want to cheat when the ref isn't looking, the problem is still there. Religion often acts like a coach, giving us lists of "do's and don'ts." While those rules are good, they don't have the power to fix the "sin virus" inside us.

We need more than just a new set of rules; we need a new heart. We need a rescue that goes deeper than our actions. If we could have saved ourselves by being good, then Jesus wouldn't have had to die on the cross. The fact that the Son of God had to come and give his life is the ultimate proof that we were in a situation we couldn't handle. We were down by a million points with no time left on the clock, and we needed a miracle.

## The Mirror of the Law

God gave us his laws, like the Ten Commandments, to act as a mirror. When you look in a mirror after a tough, muddy game, the mirror doesn't wash your face. It just shows you how dirty you are. The law shows us God's perfect standard so that we will stop trying to brag about ourselves and start looking for help. It reveals the gap between who we are and who God made us to be.

Acknowledging that you need help is actually the first step toward true strength. In a locker room, the player who hides an injury is a liability to the team. The player who admits they are hurt can get the treatment they need to get back in the game. Seeing why we need help isn't about feeling miserable; it's about being honest so that we can be healed.

## The Need for a Substitute

Since we cannot hit the mark of perfection, we need someone else to do it for us. We need a "designated hitter" who can step up to the plate and knock it out of the park every single time. We need someone who can pay the penalty for our fouls so that we don't have to be kicked out of the game forever.

This is where the story starts to get exciting. Once you realize that you are completely stuck and unable to save yourself, you are finally ready to meet the Savior. You stop looking at your own "stats" and start looking at his. You stop trying to build your own ladder to heaven and start looking for the one God sent down to us. Help is available, but you have to admit that you need it before you can receive it.

## Hope for the Injured

If you are feeling the weight of your own mistakes today, remember that God isn't surprised by your weakness. He knew you couldn't do it alone, and he never expected you to. He didn't give us a "do-it-yourself" kit for salvation. He gave us a Savior.

When you see why people need help, you stop judging others for their failures and start being thankful for God's grace. You realize that everyone is in the same boat. We are all "injured players" in need of a great Physician. This levels the playing field and makes us realize that we are all desperate for the same Hero. We were made for greatness, but we are currently broken, and that is exactly why Jesus came to find us.

# CHAPTER 4

## OWN YOUR NEED FOR A SAVIOR

In the world of sports, the hardest thing for a player to do is admit they can't handle a situation. We are coached from day one to be tough, to "grind it out," and to never show a hint of weakness to the opponent. But imagine a quarterback trying to play with a blind side he literally cannot see, or a pitcher whose arm is completely spent but refuses to call for the bullpen. If they keep pretending everything is fine, the whole team eventually pays the price.

The biggest "win" you will ever have in this life isn't a trophy or a scholarship. It is the moment you stop the act, drop the mask, and finally own the fact that you need a Savior. It's the moment you realize that "trying harder" is a dead end.

### Stepping Out of the Huddle of Excuses

We all have a "huddle" of excuses we retreat to when we mess up. When we get caught in a lie, lose our temper on the court, or let pride get the best of us, our brain immediately starts running "defensive plays." We say things like, *I'm not as bad as that kid who got suspended,* or *I only acted that way because the ref was being unfair,* or *I'm just stressed out.* We try to explain away our sin because we desperately want to believe we are still the ones in control of our destiny. But owning your need for Jesus means stepping out of that huddle of excuses and standing alone before God. It means looking at the "foul" in your own heart—the hidden thoughts, the selfishness, the times you've ignored God—and saying, "I did this. This is on me." This isn't about beating yourself up or becoming a person who walks around with their head down. It's about being truthful. You can't be rescued from a situation you won't admit you are in. You have to sign your name to the "injury report" before the Great Physician can actually start the healing process.

## The "I Can Do It Myself" Trap

The most dangerous person on any roster is the one who thinks they are bigger than the system. In our spiritual lives, we often try to be our own saviors. We tell ourselves that if we just practice more, go to church more often, or follow a list of "good person" rules, we can fix the "sin problem" through sheer willpower.

It's like trying to bail out a sinking boat with a plastic spoon. You're working incredibly hard, you're exhausted, and you might even look busy to the people watching from the shore, but you're still going down. Owning your need means dropping the spoon. It means admitting that your best effort on your best day will never be enough to reach the standard of a perfect and holy God. This is actually where true freedom starts. When you realize you can't save yourself, the crushing pressure to be perfect disappears. You stop trying to "earn" a spot on the roster and start realizing that Jesus has already bought your jersey, paid your league fees, and secured your place on the team.

## A Personal Decision, Not a Team Move

You might have grown up in a house where the Bible is read every day. Your parents might be the strongest Christians you know, and your coaches might start every practice with a prayer. That is an incredible blessing, but you cannot live on their "stats." In sports, just because your dad was a Hall of Fame legend doesn't mean you automatically get a championship ring. You have to step onto the field yourself. You have to put in the work.

Owning your need for a Savior is a deeply personal decision. It is the moment where God stops being "the God of the Bible" or "the God my family talks about" and becomes **your** Savior. It's a one-on-one conversation between you and the King. It happens when the truth hits you: if you were the only person on earth, Jesus still would have walked to the cross just for you. You have to stop hiding in the crowd and step into the light.

## The Unexpected Strength in Surrender

In our culture, the word "surrender" sounds like a total loss. It sounds like waving a white flag, hanging your head, and quitting the game. But in the Kingdom of God, surrender is the only way you actually win.

When you surrender your life to Jesus, you aren't quitting; you are switching teams. You are moving from a team that is destined to lose, the team of "Self" and "Sin", to the team that has already won the final victory: the team of "Christ."

It takes way more courage to admit you need help than it does to keep faking it. It takes a real man or woman of God to stand up and say, "I am a sinner, I've messed up, and I cannot fix myself." When you own that need, God doesn't look at you with disappointment or give you a lecture. He looks at you with open arms. The Bible is clear: God opposes the proud, but he gives grace to the humble. If you want his power in your life, you have to start with humility. You have to admit you're out of your league.

## Signing the Lifetime Contract

Think of this moment as signing your official contract with the King. When an athlete signs with a pro team, they are making a public statement: *"I am yours. I follow your playbook. I wear your colors. I trust your leadership over mine."* Owning your need for a Savior is you signing on the dotted line.

You are effectively telling God:

- **"I admit I've broken the rules."** You stop calling it "mistakes" and start calling it what God calls it: sin.
- **"I know I'm stuck."** You admit that no amount of "being a good kid" can bridge the gap between you and a holy God.
- **"I trust your work."** You believe that when Jesus died and rose again, he was doing it to pay the "fine" for your fouls.
- **"I'm handing over the ball."** You stop trying to be the MVP of your own life and you let Jesus be the Captain.

## The Shift in Your Daily Game

Once you own your need, the way you play and live starts to change. You don't have to walk around with that heavy weight of shame anymore. Your "permanent record" is wiped totally clean because Jesus' perfect record has been credited to your account.

Now, when you make a mistake, and you will, you don't have to hide in the bushes like Adam and Eve did. You can go straight to your Savior, admit the foul, and get right back in the action. You are now playing with a new kind of confidence. You aren't playing *for* love or trying to *earn* God's approval; you are playing *from* a position of being totally loved. You know you are accepted, regardless of what the scoreboard says at the end of the day. This is the foundation for everything that comes next. You have faced the problem of sin, you have owned your need, and you are finally ready to walk with the Holy Spirit.

## The Relief of Being Found

There is an old story about a sheep that gets lost and stuck in a thicket of thorns. The sheep can't get itself out; the more it struggles, the deeper the thorns go. It just has to wait for the shepherd to find it. Owning your need is like that sheep finally stopping its struggling and letting out a cry for help.

When the Shepherd finds you, he doesn't kick you for getting lost. He picks you up, puts you on his shoulders, and carries you back to the flock. That is what Jesus does when we own our need. He carries the weight that was crushing us. He brings us back to the place where we belong. You were made for greatness, and that greatness starts the moment you admit you can't reach it on your own.

# SECTION FOUR

## JOIN THE GREAT RESCUE

*Every athlete knows the feeling of being recruited. There is a moment when a coach looks at you and says, "I want you on my team." They aren't just looking at your jersey; they are looking at your potential. Throughout the first three sections of this journey, we have looked at the "pre-game." We saw how God designed a perfect world, how sin threw a wrench into the gears, and how Jesus stepped onto the field as the ultimate Hero to win back what was lost.*

*But a victory on the field doesn't mean much if you aren't actually part of the team. This fourth part is about your invitation to join the greatest rescue mission in the history of the universe. This isn't just about knowing facts about God; it's about a relationship that changes how you wake up in the morning and how you compete in the afternoon. We are moving from the sidelines into the game.*

*Over the next four chapters, we are going to explore what it looks like to actually follow Jesus. We'll talk about "Grace", the gift you didn't earn. We'll talk about "Repentance", the decision to change your direction. We'll look at how to grow into the person God created you to be, and finally, how to take this message back to your teammates, your family, and your friends. The rescue is happening, and the Captain is calling your name.*

# CHAPTER 1

## ACCEPT THE GIFT OF GRACE

Imagine you are trying out for the most elite team in the country. The standards are impossibly high. The coach is looking for a perfect 100% score on every drill. You show up, you give it everything you have, but at the end of the day, you know you didn't make the cut. You looked at the stats, and you're just not fast enough or strong enough. You're packing up your gear, feeling that heavy weight of failure, when the coach walks up to you. He hands you a team jersey with your name on it and says, "Welcome to the roster. Your spot is paid for."

You'd probably be confused. You'd say, "Coach, I didn't hit the numbers. I don't deserve this." And he would look you in the eye and say, "I know. But I'm giving it to you anyway."

That is **Grace**. In the world of sports, we are used to "merit." You get what you earn. You get playing time because you worked hard. You get a trophy because you won. But in the Kingdom of God, the most important thing you will ever receive is something you could never, ever earn.

### The Definition of the Gift

Grace is a word we hear in church all the time, but we often miss how radical it really is. Grace is "unmerited favor." That's a fancy way of saying God gives us his best when we deserve his worst. To understand grace, you have to see it alongside two other words: Justice and Mercy.

- **Justice** is getting what you deserve. If you break a rule and get a penalty, that's justice.
- **Mercy** is *not* getting the punishment you deserve. If the ref sees the foul but lets you stay in the game, that's mercy.
- **Grace** is getting a reward you *didn't* earn. It's like committing a foul, being forgiven for it, and then being handed the MVP trophy anyway.

This goes against everything we are taught on the field. We are taught that "there's no such thing as a free lunch" and that "you get out what you put in." But if we got what we put in when it comes to God, we would all be disqualified. Grace is God's way of saying that the "score" between you and Him isn't based on your performance; it's based on Jesus' performance.

## Why It Is Hard for Athletes to Accept

As an athlete, your whole life is built on performance. You are graded by your stats, your speed, and your wins. This makes accepting grace very difficult. Our pride wants to say, "I can do this myself." We want to feel like we earned our way to God. We want to be able to brag about how many chapters we read, how many times we prayed, or how "good" we are compared to the kids who get in trouble.

But the moment you try to "earn" God's love, you are stepping away from grace. Grace is a gift, and a gift can only be received, not bought. If you tried to pay your friend for a birthday present they gave you, it would be an insult. It would mean you don't want to be in their debt. We often do the same thing with God. We try to "pay him back" by being extra good. But grace says, "You can't pay me back. The price was already paid on the cross. Just take the gift."

## The Power of the "Paid-in-Full" Contract

When a professional athlete signs a "guaranteed contract," it means their pay is locked in regardless of whether they have a bad game or get an injury. They can play with a sense of security because the deal is signed.

Accepting grace is like signing a guaranteed contract with God. Your "spot on the team" doesn't depend on how you feel on a Tuesday morning or whether you stumbled and sinned on a Friday night. It depends on the finished work of Jesus. When he said "It is finished" on the cross, he was signing the contract for you.

This doesn't mean we stop trying. In fact, it should make us work harder! A player with a guaranteed contract doesn't sit on the bench and eat chips; they play with a sense of freedom and joy because they aren't afraid of being cut. When you accept grace, you stop playing for *approval* and start playing *from* a place of being already approved.

## The Mirror of Truth

To accept grace, you have to be honest about how much you need it. You have to look in the mirror and admit that you are "spiritually bankrupt." You have to realize that without Jesus, your score is zero.

This is the hardest part of the process. Our ego wants to believe we have at least a few "points" on the board. We want to think, "Sure, I'm a sinner, but I'm a *talented* sinner" or "I'm a *nice* sinner." But grace only flows to the humble. It's like a mountain: the water doesn't sit on the high, proud peaks; it flows down into the low valleys. If you want to experience the fullness of God's grace, you have to get low. You have to admit that you have nothing to offer him but your need.

## Living Under the Waterfall

Imagine God's grace as a massive waterfall in the middle of a desert. You are thirsty, tired, and covered in dust from the "game" of life. You don't have to pay to get under the water. You don't have to prove you're a "good enough" runner to deserve the water. You just have to walk into it.

Accepting grace is a daily decision. It isn't just something that happens once when you're a kid. Every morning, you have to wake up and remind yourself: "I am a child of God not because of what I did yesterday, but because of what Jesus did 2,000 years ago." This keeps you humble when you win and hopeful when you lose. It protects you from the two biggest enemies of an athlete's soul: Pride (when you think you're the greatest) and Despair (when you think you're a failure).

## Grace is Not a "Get Out of Jail Free" Card

Sometimes people hear about grace and think, "Cool, so I can just do whatever I want! If God's going to forgive me anyway, I might as well break the rules and have 'fun'."

But if you truly understand what grace cost, you would never think that way. Grace was "free" for you, but it cost Jesus everything. He had to pay the "fine" with his own life so you could get the gift. When you realize that the King of the universe died so you could be on his team, it makes you want to follow his rules more than ever. It creates a "heart of gratitude." You don't obey the Coach because you're afraid he'll kick you off the team; you obey him because you love him for letting you stay.



## The Recruiting Call

Right now, the Captain is calling you. He isn't asking for your stats. He isn't asking to see your highlight reel. He is looking at your heart and offering you the gift. He is offering you a clean slate, a new jersey, and a place in a Kingdom that will never end.

Will you stop trying to earn it? Will you drop the excuses and the pride? Accepting the gift of grace is the most "un-athletic" thing you will ever do, because it requires you to admit you can't win on your own. But it is the only way to join the Great Rescue. The jersey is held out toward you. All you have to do is take it.

# CHAPTER 2

## TURN AWAY FROM YOUR SIN

In the world of sports, there is a specific word that every player understands: **Adjustment**.

Imagine you are a pitcher, and every time you throw a fastball, the batter knocks it out of the park. Or imagine you are a soccer player, and you keep dribbling the ball into a crowd of defenders instead of passing to your open teammate. Your coach pulls you aside during a timeout and says, "You have to change what you're doing. If you keep going this way, you're going to lose the game."

At that moment, you have a choice. You can keep doing things your way, or you can "turn." You can adjust your stance, change your strategy, and head in a new direction. In the Bible, there is a special word for this kind of "about-face." It is called **Repentance**.

### What Does Repentance Really Mean?

A lot of people think that repenting just means feeling bad or crying because you got caught doing something wrong. But if you get a penalty for tripping someone and you're only sorry because the referee saw you, that's not repentance—that's just being bummed out that you got a red card!

True repentance is like being on the wrong side of the field and realizing you're running toward the wrong goal. You don't just slow down; you stop, you turn around 180 degrees, and you start sprinting toward the right goal. It's a change of mind that leads to a change of action. It means saying to God, "I've been the captain of my own life, and I've been making a mess of it. I'm turning away from my way of doing things, and I'm turning toward Your way."

## The "U-Turn" on the Field

Think of your life as a big field. Before you meet Jesus, you're usually playing for "Team Me." You want what you want, when you want it. You might be mean to a sibling because they annoyed you, or you might "fudge" the truth to your teacher to stay out of trouble. When we follow our own rules, we are heading away from God.

Repentance is the big U-turn. It's not just saying "I'm sorry" with your mouth; it's showing it with your feet. If you've been bullying a kid at school, repenting means you stop the bullying and start treating them with kindness. If you've been lazy and disrespectful to your parents, it means you turn toward being helpful and obedient. It's about changing teams. You leave "Team Me" and you join "Team Jesus."

## The "Broken Play" of Sin

In football, a "broken play" is when everything goes wrong. The quarterback trips, the receivers run the wrong routes, and the ball ends up on the ground. Sin is like a broken play for your life. It messes up your relationship with God, it hurts the people around you, and it makes you feel heavy and sad inside.

God hates sin, but not because he's a "mean ref" who wants to ruin your fun. He hates sin because he loves you, and he knows that sin is like a poison that hurts his children. Turning away from sin is like dropping a heavy backpack that has been slowing you down during your sprints. God wants you to turn away from the bad stuff so you can be free to run the race he has planned for you.

## Why Is It Hard to Turn?

Let's be honest: sometimes sin feels "fun" for a minute. It can feel good to win an argument by being mean, or to get something you want by being sneaky. That's why turning away is hard. It requires us to admit that our way of doing things is actually wrong.

In sports, it's hard to admit your technique is bad. You might have been shooting a basketball with the wrong form for years. When a coach tries to fix it, it feels weird and uncomfortable at first. You might even play worse for a day or two while you learn the new way. But if you want to be a champion, you have to trust the coach's correction. Turning away from sin feels "weird" at first because we are so used to our old, selfish habits. But as we practice following Jesus, the new way starts to feel like home.

## The Secret Ingredient: God's Kindness

You might think that God is waiting for you to get perfect before he lets you turn to him. You might think he's standing there with a scowl, crossing his arms and waiting for you to "fix yourself." But the Bible tells us a secret: it is God's **kindness** that leads us to repentance.

Imagine a coach who sees you struggling. Instead of yelling and benching you, he puts his arm around your shoulder and says, "Hey, I know you're frustrated. Let me show you a better way to play. I'm not giving up on you." How would that make you feel? It would make you *want* to change! That is exactly how God treats us. He doesn't wait for us to be perfect. He loves us right where we are, and his love gives us the courage to turn around and head home.

## You Don't Turn Alone

The coolest part about joining the Great Rescue is that you don't have to turn away from sin using only your own muscles. Remember the Holy Spirit we talked about? He is like your "Internal Coach." When you are tempted to do something wrong, he's the one who whispers to your heart, *"Hey, that's the wrong goal. Turn around!"* When you decide to repent, God gives you the power to actually do it. It's like having a turbo-boost on your U-turn. You provide the "Yes, I want to change," and God provides the strength to make the move. You aren't just trying harder; you are trusting more.

## A Daily Adjustment

Repentance isn't just something you do once when you first become a Christian. It's something we do every single day. Just like a professional golfer makes tiny adjustments to their swing every time they hit the ball, we have to check our hearts every day.

Maybe you woke up in a bad mood and were grumpy at breakfast. That's a moment to stop, pray, and turn. *"Lord, I'm sorry for being grumpy. I want to be kind today. Help me turn back to You."* This keeps your heart "clean" and keeps you close to the Captain. It prevents the small mistakes from turning into big, game-ending fouls.

## The Celebration in the Locker Room

Jesus told a story about a son who ran away and made a bunch of bad choices. When the son finally realized he was wrong, he turned around and headed back to his father. He thought his father would be angry, but instead, the father ran to him, hugged him, and threw a giant party!

Jesus says that every time one person turns away from sin and turns toward God, the angels in heaven have a massive celebration. It's like a locker room celebration after winning the Super Bowl. God isn't looking to punish you when you turn; he's looking to celebrate that his child is finally heading the right way.

## Your Move

Are you running toward the wrong goal today? Is there something in your life, a lie, a bad attitude, or a secret habit, that you know isn't part of God's plan?

Don't be afraid to turn. Don't worry about being "perfect" first. Just stop, admit it to God, and make that U-turn. The Captain is standing there with his arms open, ready to help you run the right way. When you turn away from sin, you aren't losing anything valuable; you are gaining everything that matters. You're joining the rescue. You're getting back in the game.

# CHAPTER 3

## GROW IN YOUR NEW LIFE

Think about the day you first started playing your favorite sport. Maybe you were five years old, your jersey was three sizes too big, and you spent more time looking at the grass than at the ball. You were officially on the team, but you weren't a pro yet. You had the uniform, but you didn't have the skills. To get better, you had to go through a process. You had to show up to practice, listen to the coach, and do the same drills over and over again.

Following Jesus is exactly the same way. The moment you accept God's grace and decide to follow Him, you are "on the team." Your spot is safe. But that is just the beginning of the journey. God doesn't want you to stay a "rookie" forever. He wants you to grow, to get stronger, and to become a "veteran" in your faith. In the Bible, this process is called **Sanctification**. It's a big word, but it really just means "becoming more like Jesus every day."

### The "Nutrition" of the Bible

If an athlete only eats candy and soda, they aren't going to have the energy to win a game. Their muscles will be weak, and they'll get tired in the first five minutes. To grow physically, you need good food. To grow spiritually, you need the "soul food" found in the Bible.

The Bible isn't just an old book of rules; it's God's playbook for your life. When you read it, you're letting the Coach speak directly to you. You start to learn how He thinks, what He loves, and how He wants you to handle tough situations.

Try to make it a habit to read a little bit of the Bible every day. You don't have to read ten chapters at a time. Even just a few verses can give you the "protein" you need to stay strong. When you read, ask yourself: *"What does this tell me about God?"* and *"How can I use this on the field today?"* The more you read, the more you'll start to think like a champion.

## Staying in the Huddle: Prayer

Can you imagine a quarterback who never talks to the coach? Or a goalie who ignores the rest of the defenders? The team would be a mess! Communication is the key to any winning team. In your new life with Jesus, communication is called **Prayer**.

Prayer isn't a magic spell, and it doesn't have to be fancy. It's just talking to God like He's your best friend or your favorite coach. You can pray anywhere—in the locker room before a big game, on the bus, or while you're laying in bed at night.

- **Thank Him:** "Lord, thanks for giving me the strength to play today."

- **Ask for Help:** "Coach, I'm feeling really nervous about this game. Help me to be brave."

- **Own Your Fouls:** "I'm sorry I lost my temper at practice. Help me to be a better teammate tomorrow."

When you stay in constant communication with God, you'll start to feel His peace and His guidance. You'll realize that you're never playing the game alone.

## The Power of Practice: Discipline

Nobody becomes a superstar overnight. It takes thousands of hours of practice. You have to do the "boring" stuff, like running laps or practicing your footwork, so that when the big moment comes, you're ready. Growing in your faith takes discipline, too.

Discipline means doing the right thing even when you don't feel like it. There will be days when you don't feel like being kind. There will be days when you'd rather sleep in than pray. But just like a dedicated athlete gets out of bed for a 6:00 AM practice, a follower of Jesus makes time for the things that help them grow.

Every time you choose to tell the truth when it's hard, or every time you choose to encourage a teammate instead of complaining, you are "leveling up." You are building spiritual muscles that will help you stay strong when life gets difficult.

## Don't Play Solo: The Team (Church)

You can practice by yourself in your driveway for hours, but you can't play a real game alone. You need a team. In your walk with God, that team is the **Church**.

The church isn't just a building; it's a group of people who are all heading toward the same goal. When you're part of a church or a youth group, you have teammates who can cheer you up when you're down and challenge you to be better. We need each other! Sometimes you'll be the one helping a friend understand a Bible verse, and sometimes a friend will be the one helping you through a tough week. When we stand together, we are much harder to beat.

## Handling the "Losing Streaks"

Even the best teams in the world lose sometimes. Even the best Christians mess up. You might have a week where you're grumpy, you ignore your Bible, and you say something mean. When that happens, the enemy (the devil) will whisper to you: *"See? You're not a real Christian. You haven't grown at all. You might as well just quit."*

Don't listen to that! Growth isn't a perfectly straight line up. It's more like a series of ups and downs that slowly heads higher. When you fall, don't stay down. Admit your mistake to God, accept His grace (remember Chapter 1?), and get back to practice. A "loss" is only a total failure if you refuse to learn from it and keep going.

## Watching for the "Fruit"

How do you know if you're actually growing? In an apple tree, you look for apples. In a follower of Jesus, you look for what the Bible calls the **Fruit of the Spirit**.

As you grow, you'll notice that you are becoming more loving, joyful, peaceful, patient, kind, good, faithful, gentle, and self-controlled. You'll realize that you don't get as angry as you used to when things don't go your way. You'll find yourself wanting to help others more than you want to help yourself. That is the Holy Spirit working in you! It's like seeing your "stats" improve over the course of a season. It's proof that the Coach is doing a great work in your heart.

Growth takes time. You won't be a spiritual giant by next Tuesday. It's a "long game" that lasts your whole life. The goal isn't to be perfect; the goal is to be closer to Jesus today than you were yesterday.

So, keep showing up. Keep "eating" the Word. Keep talking to the Coach. Keep leaning on your teammates. You are part of the Great Rescue, and God is committed to helping you grow into the incredible person He designed you to be. You're not just an athlete anymore; you're a child of the King, and your future is brighter than any championship trophy!

# CHAPTER 4

## SPREAD THE MESSAGE OF HOPE

Imagine you've spent your whole life practicing on a court with broken rims and flat balls. Then, one day, a scout shows up and brings you to a state-of-the-art stadium. The grass is perfect, the equipment is brand new, and the Coach is the greatest to ever live. Not only that, but he tells you that your spot is guaranteed and the snacks are free. What is the very first thing you're going to do? You aren't going to sit in the dugout and keep it to yourself. You're going to run back to your old neighborhood, find all your friends who are still struggling with those flat basketballs, and say, "You won't believe what I found! There's a place for you here, too!"

That is the heart of spreading the message of hope. In the Bible, this is often called **The Great Commission**. It sounds like a heavy, formal term, but in sports language, it's simply the "Post-Game Interview" that lasts for the rest of your life. It's the moment the Coach gives you the playbook and says, "The rescue is for everyone. Now, go and get the rest of the team."

### The Strategy: Living as a Human Billboard

In the world of professional sports, companies pay millions of dollars to put their logos on jerseys. Why? Because they know that if you admire an athlete, you'll look at what they're wearing. You are a "brand ambassador" for the Kingdom of God. Before you ever open your mouth to talk about a Bible verse, people are reading the "logo" of your life.

Think about the high-pressure moments of a game. When the referee makes a call that is clearly wrong—a call that might cost you the game—how do you react? If you blow up, scream, and throw your helmet, you're sending a message. But if you show self-control, even when it hurts, you're sending a different message. People start to wonder, *"What does he have that I don't? Why isn't he falling apart right now?"*

Being a "Human Billboard" means your character becomes the advertisement for God's grace. It means being the hardest worker on the field, not because you're trying to show off, but because you're playing for a higher King. It means being the person who stays late to help the manager pick up the cones, or the one who sits with the new kid on the bench who doesn't have any friends yet. These small, daily actions create "curiosity." They earn you the right to be heard when you finally do speak.

## Developing Your "Scouting Report" (Your Testimony)

Every great player has a scouting report—a summary of where they came from, what their strengths are, and how they play the game. In your spiritual life, your scouting report is your **Testimony**. This is simply the story of your journey with Jesus.

A lot of kids think, *"My story is boring. I wasn't a bank robber who became a preacher. I'm just a middle-schooler who likes baseball."* But here is a secret: your story is exactly what someone else needs to hear. Most people aren't looking for a movie-star miracle; they are looking for a reason to have peace when they fail a math test or lose a championship game.

To build your testimony, think of it in three "quarters":

1. **First Quarter: The Need.** What was your life like before you really understood God's love? Maybe you felt like you had to be perfect to be loved. Maybe you were really lonely or had a quick temper.

2. **Second Quarter: The Turn.** How did you realize you needed a Savior? Was it a talk with a coach, a verse you read, or just a feeling in your heart that there had to be more to life?

3. **Third Quarter: The New Life.** How is your life different now? You still have problems, and you still lose games, but what has changed on the *inside*? Do you have more joy? Is it easier to forgive people?

When you share your story, you aren't giving a lecture. You're just sharing your "highlight reel." You are saying, "I was lost on the field, I found the Coach, and now I'm part of the rescue."

## The "Invite" Play: Breaking the Ice

Sometimes, we think spreading the message means standing on a table in the cafeteria and shouting. While that's brave, it's usually not the most effective way to reach your teammates. Most "recruiting" happens in the quiet moments—on the back of the bus, in the weight room, or while you're stretching before practice.

The "Invite" Play is simple. It's about looking for "openings" in a conversation.

- **The "Me Too" Opening:** If a teammate says, "I'm so stressed about this season," you can say, "Man, I totally get that. I used to feel the same way until I started realize that my value isn't just in my stats. My church group talks about this stuff—you should come with me sometime."

- **The "Prayer" Opening:** If someone is going through a hard time, like a divorce in their family or an injury, you can simply say, "I'm really sorry you're going through that. I'm going to be praying for you." Most people—even if they don't believe in God yet—will be touched that you care enough to pray.

- **The "Question" Opening:** Sometimes, just asking a question is the best way. "Do you ever think about God or what happens after we die?" This isn't being pushy; it's being curious.

## Handling the "Benchings" and Rejections

In sports, you're going to get rejected. You're going to try out for a team and get cut. You're going to take a shot and miss. The same thing happens when you share the message of hope. Some people will think it's "weird." Some people might make a joke at your expense.

When this happens, you have to remember the "Final Score." You aren't responsible for how people respond; you are only responsible for being a faithful messenger. If someone says "no" to an invite, it doesn't mean you failed. It just means the "timing" wasn't right. God is the one who does the heavy lifting of changing people's hearts. Your job is just to keep the door open. Stay kind. Don't get defensive. If you stay a great teammate even after they say "no," you're proving that your love for them isn't "fake." It shows them that you care about *them*, not just about "winning an argument."

## Teamwork: Building a Huddle

You shouldn't try to be a lone scout. The Great Commission is a team effort. If there are other Christians on your team or in your school, find them! There is incredible power in a "Huddle."

Think about starting a small group before practice once a week. It doesn't have to be long—just ten minutes. Read one verse, talk about how it applies to your sport, and pray for your team. When other players see a group of athletes who are united, disciplined, and full of joy, they will naturally want to know what's going on. A "Huddle" provides a safe place for people to ask questions and see that following Jesus isn't just for "quiet people"—it's for competitors, too.

## The Global Rescue: Looking Beyond the Field

While your primary "mission field" is your current team, the message of hope is meant for the whole world. Part of spreading the message is caring about what God is doing in other places.

Maybe your team can do a service project together, like cleaning up a local park or volunteering at a food bank. Maybe you can save up some of your own money to help support a missionary who is bringing the message of hope to a country where people have never heard of Jesus. When you look beyond your own "stats" and start caring about the "global score," your heart gets bigger. You realize that you are part of a massive, worldwide movement of rescue.

## Dealing with the "I'm Not Good Enough" Fear

The biggest reason kids don't share their faith is that they feel like "hypocrites." They think, *"I can't tell people about Jesus because I just got a yellow card for yelling at the ref last week,"* or *"I'm not a perfect student, so they won't listen to me."*

Here is the truth: **The world doesn't need to see a perfect Christian; they need to see a forgiven one.** If you pretend to be perfect, people will find you annoying and fake. But if you are honest about your mistakes, if you go to a teammate and say, "Hey, I'm sorry I was a jerk at practice yesterday; I'm still learning how to let God control my temper", that is incredibly powerful. It shows people that Christianity isn't a "club for perfect people." It's a "hospital for the broken." Your honesty about your struggles is actually one of your best tools for spreading hope.

## The Power of Words (and the Silence)

The Bible says that the tongue has the power of life and death. As an athlete, your words carry weight. You can use your words to "trash talk" and tear people down, or you can use them to "speak life."

Spreading the message of hope means being the person who speaks up for the kid who is being bullied. It means being the one who shuts down gossip in the locker room. It means using your social media to post things that encourage others rather than just showing off your own highlights. Every time you use your words for good, you are pushing back the darkness and letting the light of the Kingdom shine through.

## The Finish Line: Why We Do It

Why do we go through the trouble of sharing this message? Because we know the "Final Score" of history. We know that Jesus is coming back to fix everything. We know that there is a real Heaven and a real Hell, and we want as many people as possible to be on the winning team.

When you stand at the end of your life, you won't be thinking about how many points you scored in eighth grade. You'll be thinking about the people you helped. You'll be thinking about the teammate who started going to church because of you, or the friend who found hope in their darkest hour because you shared your story.

So, what is your next play?

1.  **Identify your "Target":** Who is one person on your team or in your life who needs hope right now?

2.  **Pray for the Opening:** Ask God to give you a chance to say something encouraging or to share a piece of your story.

3.  **Be Ready:** Keep your "jersey" clean. Live in a way that makes people curious about your Captain.

4.  **Speak Up:** When the moment comes, don't be afraid. The Holy Spirit will give you the words to say.

You are part of the Great Rescue. You aren't just an athlete; you are a messenger of the King. The world is full of people who are playing on flat courts with broken hearts. You know where the Great Stadium is. You know the Coach. Now, go and bring them home.

# CONCLUSION

## LIVE FOR THE GLORY OF GOD

You have reached the end of the manual, but in the Kingdom of God, the finish line of one season is always the starting blocks for the next. We have journeyed through the architecture of the universe, the tragedy of the fall, the rescue of the Cross, and the power of the Spirit. Now, we face the most important question any competitor can ask: **"Now what?"**

How do you take these truths into a locker room that smells like sweat and echoes with trash talk? How do you hold onto your faith when you're exhausted, your muscles are screaming, and you just lost the biggest game of your life? The answer is found in a single, life-altering phrase: **Living for the glory of God.**

### Pillar 1: The Definition of the Goal

In sports, "glory" is usually something we try to steal for ourselves. We want the highlight reel to be about us. We want the "likes" on social media. We want the scholarship. But the Bible tells us that glory belongs to God alone. The word "glory" in the original Hebrew is *kavod*, which literally means "heaviness" or "weight."

When you live for God's glory, you are telling the world that God is the "Heaviest" thing in your life. He carries more weight than your coach's opinion, more weight than the scouts' reports, and even more weight than your own feelings of success or failure.

### The Mirror Principle

Imagine a mirror. A mirror is a wonderful tool, but it has no light of its own. If you put a mirror in a pitch-black room, it shows nothing. But if you hold that mirror up to the sun, it becomes blindingly bright. It reflects the sun's glory into the dark corners of the world.

You are that mirror. You aren't the Sun. You aren't the source of the talent, the breath in your lungs, or the beating of your heart. Your job as a Christian athlete is to "reflect" the greatness of the Creator. When people see your hard work, your integrity, and your kindness, they shouldn't just think, *"Wow, he's a great player."* They should think, *"Wow, his God must be incredible."*

## Pillar 2: The Psychology of a God-Centered Competitor

Most athletes are driven by a "Performance Identity." This means their happiness is tied to their stats. If they score, they feel like a king. If they miss, they feel like a failure. This is a roller coaster that eventually breaks everyone.

### Playing from Victory, Not for Victory

Living for God's glory changes your "Why." You no longer play to *get* an identity; you play *from* an identity.

- **The Old Way:** "I need to win so that I am worthy of love."
- **The New Way:** "I am already perfectly loved by the King of the Universe; therefore, I can play with total freedom."

This freedom is your greatest competitive advantage. An athlete who isn't afraid to lose is the most dangerous person on the field. Why? Because they aren't "tight." They aren't choked by anxiety. They can take the big shot or make the risky play because they know their "Final Score" is already settled in Heaven.

How does a "Glory-First" athlete handle the "Dirty" side of sports? We live in a world that says, *"It's only a foul if the ref sees it,"* or *"If you aren't cheating, you aren't trying."*

### Integrity in the Dark

Living for God's glory means recognizing that there are no "secret" plays. God sees the way you talk to the bench players when the coach isn't listening. He sees the way you handle yourself in the bottom of a pile-up.

A "Glory-First" athlete values **Integrity** over **Image**.

- **Image** is who people *think* you are based on your stats and your social media.
- **Integrity** is who you *actually* are when the cameras are off and the stands are empty.

When you refuse to cheat, even when it would guarantee a win, you are saying that God's approval matters more than a trophy. That is how you make God look "Heavy" and "Important."



Many people think that "God stuff" only happens when you're praying or in church. But God is the one who created your muscles, your tendons, and your nervous system. He is the one who designed the laws of physics that allow a ball to curve or a runner to accelerate.

### Training as Worship

Every rep in the weight room can be a prayer. Every mile you run can be an act of gratitude. When you push your body to its limits, you are honoring the "Equipment" God gave you.

- **Laziness** is a form of ingratitude. It's like being given a Ferrari and letting it rust in the rain.
- **Excellence** is a form of worship. It's saying, *"God, You gave me this body and this opportunity, and I'm going to use it to the max to show how great Your creation is."*

This doesn't mean you have to be the best in the world. It means you have to be the best *you* that God created you to be.

## Pillar 5: Dealing with Injuries and Setbacks

One of the hardest parts of being an athlete is when the "game" is taken away from you. An injury can feel like a death. It can feel like God has forgotten you.

### The Glory in the Waiting Room

If you can only glorify God when you're winning, your god is actually your own success. But if you can glorify God while sitting on the sidelines with an ice pack on your knee, you have found the real secret.

In the "Waiting Room" of an injury, God is often doing a deeper work. He is teaching you that you are more than just an athlete. He is teaching you to find your joy in Him, not in your jersey. When your teammates see you staying positive and encouraging them even when you can't play, you are providing a testimony that is more powerful than a thousand touchdowns. You are showing them that your hope is "unshakeable."

## Pillar 6: The Community of the Kingdom

Sports can be a very lonely world. It's all about "me" and "my" career. But as we saw in section 4, we are called to a "Huddle."

### Being a "Great Commission" Teammate

You aren't on your team by accident. God didn't just "luck" you into that roster. You are a missionary in a jersey.

- **The Servant Leader:** Jesus said that the greatest in the kingdom is the servant of all. Be the player who picks up the equipment. Be the one who stays late to help a struggling teammate.

- **The Truth-Speaker:** Have the courage to speak up when something wrong is happening. If there's bullying or "locker room talk" that degrades people, be the one who says, *"We're better than that."*

## Pillar 7: The Final Whistle

Every career ends. Whether it ends in high school, college, or the pros, the day will come when you hang up your cleats for the last time.

**Playing for the Eternal Trophy**

If you live for the glory of God, you never have to fear the "End." You aren't playing for a trophy that will gather dust or a record that will be broken. You are playing for a Crown of Life that lasts forever.

When you get to the end of your life, the goal is to look back and see a trail of people who were helped, a legacy of integrity, and a heart that stayed close to the Coach. You want to hear those words: *"Well done, good and faithful servant."*

## Final Call to Action

The world is full of "Regular" athletes. The world is full of people who play for themselves. But the world is starving for "Resurrection Athletes."

- Be the player who loves the unlovable.
- Be the player who is honest when it costs them.
- Be the player who works harder than everyone else because they're playing for a King.

The "Great Rescue" is happening right now. It's happening in your school, in your gym, and on your field. You have the playbook. You have the Holy Spirit. You have the Captain on your side.

**Now, get out there and live for the glory of God.**

# EXTRA CONTENT
## THE JUNIOR THEOLOGIAN'S ACTION MANUAL

### Putting the "Big Truths" to Work

Systematic Theology is like a blueprint. A blueprint is a beautiful drawing of a house, but you can't live inside a piece of paper. You have to take the instructions on that paper and start laying bricks, installing windows, and turning on the lights.

This section shows you how to "live inside" the truth. We are going to look at five major "rooms" of theology and see how to put them into action right now.

### Room 1: The Doctrine of God (Theology Proper)

**Topic: The Omniscience and Omnipresence of God**

**The Big Idea:** God knows everything (Omniscience) and is everywhere at the same time (Omnipresence).

## 1. The "Secret Truth" Action

Have you ever felt like nobody really "gets" you? Maybe you're sad, but you don't have the words to explain why. Or maybe you did something really kind, but nobody saw it.

- **In Action:** Because God is Omniscient, He is the only person who knows exactly how you feel. You never have to explain yourself to Him. When you're lonely, you can say, "God, You know exactly how I feel, and You are right here with me."
- **The Practice:** Spend five minutes tonight talking to God about your "secrets"—not just the bad things, but the dreams and the quiet thoughts you have. Knowing He is already there makes prayer feel less like a speech and more like a conversation with a friend who already knows the ending of your sentences.

## 2. The "Fear-Fighter" Action

When the lights are off and the house is quiet, it's easy to feel small and afraid. But Theology Proper tells us God has no "edges."

- **In Action:** Omnipresence means God isn't "watching from a distance." He is closer to you than your own shadow.
- **The Practice:** Memorize **Psalm 139:7-10**. Next time you feel nervous, whether it's a dark room or a big test, remind yourself: "There is nowhere I can go where God is not."

## Room 2: The Doctrine of Man (Anthropology)

**Topic: The Imago Dei (The Image of God)**

**The Big Idea:** Every human being is a "mirror" designed to reflect God's glory.

## 1. The "Dignity" Action

In middle school, it's easy to judge people by what they wear, how smart they are, or how good they are at sports. But Anthropology tells us that every person is a "Masterpiece" because they carry God's image.

- **In Action:** This changes how you treat the kid who sits alone at lunch or the neighbor who seems "weird." You don't be nice to them because you're a "good person"; you be nice to them because you are respecting the Artist who made them.

- **The Practice:** The "Masterpiece Mission." This week, find one person who is usually ignored. Look them in the eye and say "Hello" or ask them a question. Remind yourself: *"This person is a living, breathing reflection of the King."*

## 2. The "Self-Worth" Action

Sometimes we look in the mirror and don't like what we see. We wish we were taller, thinner, or faster.

- **In Action:** If you are an Image-Bearer, your value doesn't come from your "stats." It comes from your "Designer."
- **The Practice:** Write down three things you *can* do (like drawing, listening, or being funny). Next to them, write how those things reflect God (He is the Ultimate Creator, the Ultimate Listener, the Creator of Joy).

## Room 3: The Doctrine of Christ (Christology)

**Topic: The Prophet, Priest, and King**

**The Big Idea:** Jesus is our perfect Teacher (Prophet), our Helper (Priest), and our Leader (King).

### 1. The "Advice" Action (Jesus as Prophet)

When you have a big decision to make, like whether to tell the truth when it's hard, you need a Prophet to tell you God's words.

- **In Action:** Instead of just asking your friends what they think, go to the "Head Prophet."
- **The Practice:** Open your Bible to the "Red Letters" (the words of Jesus). Find one thing Jesus said about being honest or kind. That is your "Direct Order" for the day.

### 2. The "Brave" Action (Jesus as King)

Sometimes we feel like the "bad guys" (sin, bullies, or scary thoughts) are winning.

- **In Action:** Because Jesus is King, He is in charge of the whole universe. He has already defeated the biggest enemies (Sin and Death).
- **The Practice:** When you feel overwhelmed, picture a King on a throne who is also your best friend. Tell Him, "King Jesus, please handle this problem for me. I'm on Your team."

**Topic: Justification and Adoption**

**The Big Idea:** God declares us "Not Guilty" (Justification) and makes us His children (Adoption).

### 1. The "Fresh Start" Action

When you mess up, like losing your temper or lying, you might feel like a "failure." You might want to hide from God.

- **In Action:** Justification means God has already looked at your "record" and written **PAID** in big red letters because of Jesus.

- **The Practice:** The "Eraser Prayer." When you sin, don't wait three days to pray. Go to God immediately. Confess it, and then *believe* that it is gone. Don't keep carrying the guilt around. A justified person walks with their head up!

### 2. The "Family" Action

A lot of kids feel like they have to "earn" their parents' or teachers' love by being good.

- **In Action:** Adoption means God is your Father forever. You didn't "earn" your way into His family, so you can't "lose" your way out of it by having a bad day.

- **The Practice:** Every morning this week, say out loud: "I am a child of the King, and He is proud of me today." See how that changes your confidence!

## Room 5: The Doctrine of the Church (Ecclesiology)

**Topic: The Body of Christ**

**The Big Idea:** We are all different parts of one "Body," and we need each other.

### 1. The "No-Jealousy" Action

When you see a friend get a new bike or get an "A" on a test, it's easy to feel jealous.

- **In Action:** If the "Hand" wins a trophy, the "Foot" should celebrate too, because they are on the same body!

- **The Practice:** The "Teammate Cheer." This week, when something good happens to someone else, be the first person to tell them "Great job!" without wishing it had happened to you.

## 2. The "Helping Hand" Action

You might think you're "too young" to help the church.

- **In Action:** Every part of the body has a job. If the pinky finger stopped working, the hand would be weaker.

- **The Practice:** Ask your parents or your church leader: "Is there one small thing I can do to help this week?" It could be picking up trash, holding a door, or writing a "Get Well" card to someone who is sick.

## Room 6: The Junior Theologian's "Daily Briefing"

To stay sharp, a Theologian needs a daily routine. Here is a 5-minute plan to keep your "System" running smoothly:

1. **The Look Up (1 Minute):** Remind yourself of one Attribute of God. ("God, You are Immutable. You never change.")

2. **The Look In (1 Minute):** Be honest about your "Humanity." ("I am a sinner, and I need Your grace today.")

3. **The Look at Christ (1 Minute):** Thank Jesus for His "Offices." ("Thank You for being my Priest and praying for me.")

4. **The Look Out (2 Minutes):** Treat someone like an "Image-Bearer." (Think of one person you will be kind to today.)

## Summary for the Junior Theologian

Theology isn't a dusty book on a high shelf. It is the "software" that runs your life. When you understand **who God is**, **who you are**, and **what Jesus did**, the world stops being a confusing place. You start to see the "Logic of Love" everywhere.

You are no longer just a kid living day-to-day. You are a **Theologian in Training**, helping God build His kingdom right where you are: in your school, in your living room, and in your heart.

# EXTRA CONTENT

# THE JUNIOR THEOLOGIAN'S GUIDE TO BIG EMOTIONS

## How Your Feelings Fit Into God's Big Plan

Have you ever felt like your emotions are a wild roller coaster? One minute you're at the top, laughing and feeling like you can conquer the world (Joy). The next minute, you're plunging down into a dark tunnel because someone said something mean (Sadness), or your heart is racing because you're worried about a big presentation at school (Fear).

As a Junior Theologian, you might wonder: *"Does God care about my feelings? Are some emotions 'sinful'? Why did God even give us feelings if they hurt so much sometimes?"*

Theology teaches us that God is the **Author of Emotions**. He isn't a robot, and He didn't design you to be one either. Because you are made in the **Image of God**, your ability to feel deeply is actually a gift.

However, because of the **Fall**, our "Feeling-Thermometer" is sometimes broken. This section will help you understand how to handle your "Big Feelings" using the blueprint of Systematic Theology.

## 1. The Theology of Joy (Reflecting God's Happiness)

**The Big Idea:** God is the happiest Being in the universe, and He made you to find your ultimate joy in Him.

In Systematic Theology, we learn about God's **Beatitude**. That's a fancy word that means God is perfectly happy and satisfied within Himself. When you feel a burst of joy because you're playing with a puppy, eating your favorite ice cream, or finishing a hard project, you are reflecting a tiny bit of God's own happiness.

- **The Problem:** Because of sin, we often try to find joy in things that don't last. We think, "If I just get that new video game, I'll be happy forever." But that joy eventually fades.

- **The Action Manual:** Junior Theologians practice **Gratitude**. Instead of just enjoying the "gift," we look up at the "Giver."

- **The Practice:** The "Joy-Trace." When you feel happy today, stop and "trace" that feeling back to God. Say, "God, thank You for this fun moment. Thank You that You are the source of all good things!"

## 2. The Theology of Sadness (God's Heart for a Broken World)

**The Big Idea:** Sadness is not a "bad" emotion; it is a sign that we know the world is not the way God originally designed it to be.

Did you know that Jesus cried? In the Gospel of John, when His friend Lazarus died, the Bible says, "Jesus wept." This is a huge theological truth! It means that God is not "above" our sadness. He is a **High Priest** who can sympathize with our weaknesses.

- **The Problem:** Sometimes sadness can make us want to hide from God or think that He is being mean.

- **The Action Manual:** Junior Theologians use **Lament**. Lament is a "prayer in the rain." It is talking to God about your sadness instead of just sitting in it.

- **The Practice:** The "Honest Prayer." If you are sad, tell God exactly why. *"God, my heart hurts because my friend moved away. I know You are a Comforter. Please hold me close today."*

### 3. The Theology of Anger (The Defense of What is Right)

**The Big Idea:** Anger was designed to be our "Alarm System" against things that are wrong and unjust.

In Theology Proper, we learn about **God's Holy Wrath**. God gets angry at sin, bullying, and lies because those things hurt the people He loves. Anger, in its purest form, is meant to make us want to fix what is broken.

- **The Problem:** Because of our "Total Depravity," our anger usually turns into **Sinful Anger**. We get mad because we didn't get our way, or we want to hurt someone back. This is called "Selfish Anger."

- **The Action Manual:** Junior Theologians practice **Self-Control** (a Fruit of the Spirit). Before you react in anger, ask yourself: *"Am I mad because God's rules were broken, or just because I'm not getting my way?"*

- **The Practice:** The "Cool-Down Countdown." When you feel the "heat" of anger, stop and count to ten while saying, *"God is the Judge, not me."* This gives your heart a second to switch from "Selfish Anger" to "Seeking Justice."

### 4. The Theology of Fear (Trusting the Sovereignty of God)

**The Big Idea:** Fear is a reminder that we are small and that we need a Protector who is much bigger than we are.

Systematic Theology teaches us about God's **Sovereignty**. This means God is in total control of every atom and every second of time. Fear happens when we forget who is on the throne. We feel like the world is "out of control," and we are afraid of what might happen.

- **The Problem:** Fear can paralyze us. It can make us stop doing the good things God has called us to do.

- **The Action Manual:** Junior Theologians practice **Trust**. We don't try to "stop feeling afraid"; we just "start trusting the King."

- **The Practice:** The "Scripture Shield." Choose one verse about God's power (like **Joshua 1:9**). When fear knocks on your door, answer it with that verse. Say, *"I am afraid, but my God is Sovereign, and He is with me."*

## 5. The Theology of Peace (The Result of Justification)

**The Big Idea:** Peace is not just the "absence of trouble"; it is the "presence of God."

Because of **Justification**, we have "Peace with God." The war between us and God is over! This theological truth should create a deep, quiet sense of "okay-ness" in our hearts, even when the world outside is noisy.

- **The Problem:** We often think peace comes from having a perfect life with no homework and no chores. That is "False Peace."
- **The Action Manual:** Junior Theologians practice **Stillness**.
- **The Practice:** The "Bedtime Hand-Off." Every night, imagine you are holding all your big feelings in your hands like a heavy bag. In your mind, "hand" that bag to Jesus. Say, *"Lord, You are in charge of tomorrow. I'm going to rest in Your peace."*

## Putting it All Together: The Heart-Check

To keep your emotions in line with your theology, try the **Junior Theologian Heart-Check** once a day. Ask yourself these three questions:

1. **What am I feeling?** (Identify the emotion: Joy, Sad, Mad, or Scared).
2. **What is the truth?** (Remind yourself of a Doctrine: God is in control, God is Love, or God is the Judge).
3. **What is my move?** (Decide to Praise, Lament, Forgive, or Trust).

When you do this, your feelings stop being your "boss" and start being your "servant." They help you see God more clearly. You aren't just a kid with "moods"; you are a child of God learning to feel the way your Father feels.

# EXTRA CONTENT
## THE GREAT SYSTEMATIC THEOLOGY MEGA-QUIZ

**Level: Junior Theologian Certification**

Congratulations! You have traveled through the most important truths in the universe. You've looked at the blueprint of creation, the rescue mission of Jesus, and the action plan for your feelings. But how much of that "System" stayed in your brain?

It's time to put your knowledge to the test. This isn't a boring school test; it's a **Scouting Report** for your soul. Grab a piece of paper, find a quiet spot, and let's see if you're ready for your Junior Theologian Certification! *(Read until the end to get your answers!)*

*In this level, we test what you know about God's Nature and our Design.*

**1. The "I AM" Mystery** When God told Moses His name was "I AM WHO I AM," what was He teaching us about Himself?

- A) That He is forgetful and couldn't remember His name.
- B) That He is "Self-Existent" (Aseity) and doesn't need anything else to live.
- C) That He only likes short names.
- D) That He is a mystery that no one can ever talk to.

**2. True or False: The Changing God** God sometimes changes His mind about His promises if we have a really bad day.

**3. The Attribute Match-Up** Match the "Big Word" on the left with its kid-friendly definition on the right:

| | |
|---|---|
| **1. Omniscience** | A. God is everywhere at the same time. |
| **2. Omnipotence** | B. God never, ever changes. |
| **3. Omnipresence** | C. God knows every fact and every thought. |
| **4. Immutability** | D. God has all the power in the universe. |

**4. The "Imago Dei" Detective** If you see a classmate being teased because they are different from everyone else, which doctrine should pop into your head to tell you that bullying is wrong?

A) The Doctrine of Sleep.

B) The Doctrine of the Image of God (Imago Dei).

C) The Doctrine of Clouds.

D) The Doctrine of Math.

**5. The Ink in the Water** In Chapter 2, we talked about "Total Depravity." What does that mean for us?

A) We are as mean and bad as we could possibly be.

B) We are 100% perfect.

C) Sin has touched every part of us (mind, heart, and body), like ink in a glass of water.

D) We only sin when we are hungry.

*In this level, we see if you understand the "Person and Work" of Jesus.*

**6. The 100/100 Rule** Theology teaches us about the "Hypostatic Union." This means Jesus is:

    A) 50% God and 50% Man.

    B) 100% God and 100% Man at the same time.

    C) A man who worked really hard until God made Him a god.

    D) An angel wearing a human costume.

**7. The Three Offices** Jesus has three "jobs" or "offices." Which one describes Jesus as the one who speaks God's words to us perfectly?

    A) The King.

    B) The Priest.

    C) The Prophet.

    D) The Principal.

**8. Scenario Challenge: The Scared Heart** Imagine you are very afraid of something that might happen next week. If you remember that Jesus is your **King**, how does that help you?

    A) It reminds me that I should buy a crown.

    B) It reminds me that Jesus is in control of the whole universe and is stronger than my fear.

    C) It reminds me that I should try to be my own king.

    D) It doesn't help at all.

**9. The Priest's Job** In the Old Testament, a Priest offered sacrifices for the people. How did Jesus fulfill the "Office of Priest"?

    A) He built a giant temple out of gold.

    B) He offered Himself as the perfect sacrifice to pay for our sins.

    C) He told everyone to be nicer to each other.

    D) He became a judge in a courtroom.

*In this level, we check your knowledge of how we are saved and how the Church works.*

**10. The Great Exchange** In the "Action Manual," we learned about Justification. What is the "Great Exchange"?

> A) Trading your old bike for a new one.

> B) Jesus taking our sin and giving us His perfect righteousness.

> C) Trading lunch snacks at school.

> D) God taking our good deeds and giving us a trophy.

**11. Adoption Papers** Because of salvation, God becomes our "Father." This is called "Adoption." What is one benefit of being adopted into God's family?

> A) You never have to do chores again.

> B) You are a child of the King, and you can't "lose" your place in the family.

> C) You get to move to a castle tomorrow.

> D) You are better than everyone else who isn't adopted.

**12. The Body of Christ Puzzle** If the "Eye" in the church is jealous of the "Hand," which theological truth are they forgetting?

> A) That they should both try to be feet.

> B) That every part of the Body of Christ is important and has a special job to do.

> C) That hands are better than eyes.

> D) That they should stop being part of the body.

**13. True or False: The Building is the Church** If a church building burns down, the Church is gone.

*In this level, we test your knowledge of the "Heart" and the "End."*

**14. The Emotion Alarm** According to the "Theology of Emotions," what was **Anger** originally designed to do?

    A) Make us feel powerful and scary.

    B) Act as an "Alarm System" against things that are wrong and unjust.

    C) Help us win arguments with our parents.

    D) It was a mistake; God didn't mean to give us anger.

**15. The "God-Centered" Happy** If you are happy today because you are playing outside, what is the Junior Theologian's "move"?

    A) To forget about God and just keep playing.

    B) To "Trace" the joy back to the Giver and thank God for the happiness.

    C) To feel guilty for being happy.

    D) To ask for five more hours of playtime.

**16. The Resurrection Hope** When Jesus returns, what will happen to the bodies of those who trust Him?

    A) They will stay in the ground forever.

    B) They will be raised as "Glorified Bodies" that never get sick, old, or hurt.

    C) They will turn into ghosts and fly on clouds.

    D) They will look exactly the same as they do now.

**17. The New Earth Mystery** What is the "New Heavens and New Earth" going to be like?

    A) A boring place where we just sing songs for a million years.

    B) A renewed, perfect world where we live, work, and play with God face-to-face.

    C) A place where there is no gravity.

    D) It is just a dream; it isn't really going to happen.

*In this final level, you must apply "Big Truths" to "Big Problems."*

**18. The "Secret Sin" Problem** Imagine you did something wrong, and nobody—not your parents, your teachers, or your friends—saw you do it. Which attribute of God tells you that you should still confess it?

    A) God's Immutability.

    B) God's Omniscience (He knows everything).

    C) God's Beatitude (His happiness).

    D) God's Creation of the stars.

**19. The "I'm Not Good Enough" Problem** If you feel like God is mad at you because you failed a test or weren't "perfect," which doctrine reminds you that you are safe?

    A) The Doctrine of Justification (God already declared me "Not Guilty").

    B) The Doctrine of the Sun and Moon.

    C) The Doctrine of Fasting.

    D) The Doctrine of Church Buildings.

**20. The "Unkind Neighbor" Problem** If someone in your neighborhood is very mean and grumpy, why should you still treat them with respect?

    A) Because you want them to give you candy.

    B) Because they are an Image-Bearer of God, and God loves them.

    C) Because you are afraid of them.

    D) Because your mom told you to.

# THE JUNIOR THEOLOGIAN'S ANSWER KEY & DEEP-DIVE EXPLANATION

*(Read this section carefully! Even if you got the answer right, the "Why" is the most important part!)*

## Level 1 Answers: The Blueprint

**1. Answer: B (God is Self-Existent/Aseity) Explanation:** This is a huge building block of theology. Most things in the world need something else. A fire needs oxygen. A plant needs dirt. You need lunch. But God is the only "Uncaused Cause." He is the "I AM." He is the Boss of the universe because He is the only one who doesn't owe His life to anyone else. This should make us feel very safe! If God needed us, He might get tired of us. But since He doesn't need us, it means He loves us just because He *wants* to.

**2. Answer: False Explanation:** This is the doctrine of **Immutability**. In a world where your favorite toy breaks, your friends might move away, and your clothes get too small, God is the "Rock." He says in the Bible, "I the Lord do not change." His promises are like a contract that can never be broken. If He promised to love you in the Bible, He will never "change His mind" because you had a bad day.

**3. Answer: 1-C, 2-D, 3-A, 4-B Explanation:** * **Omniscience** (All-knowing) means God has the ultimate "Google" in His head.

- **Omnipotence** (All-powerful) means God's "batteries" never run out.
- **Omnipresence** (Everywhere) means God doesn't have a car because He's already where the car is going!
- **Immutability** (Unchanging) means God is the same yesterday, today, and forever.

**4. Answer: B (Imago Dei) Explanation:** This is the theology of "Human Value." Every single person, the kid who is hard to get along with, the person who looks different, and even your "enemy", is a masterpiece designed by God. When we are mean to people, we are actually being mean to God's artwork. A Junior Theologian sees the "hidden crown" on everyone's head.

**5. Answer: C (Total Depravity) Explanation:** This is the theology of "The Problem." We aren't just "kind of" messy; we are "Totally Depraved." This doesn't mean we are as bad as we could be (God's grace keeps us from that!), but it means sin is in our thoughts, our words, and our bodies. This is why we need a Savior, we can't just "try harder" to be good, we need a new heart!

## Level 2 Answers: The Hero

**6. Answer: B (100% God and 100% Man) Explanation:** This is the **Hypostatic Union**. It is the most important math in the world! If Jesus were only God, He couldn't die for us. If He were only Man, His death wouldn't be powerful enough to save everyone. He had to be both to be the "Bridge" between Heaven and Earth.

**7. Answer: C (The Prophet) Explanation:** A **Prophet** is a messenger. In the old days, prophets said "Thus saith the Lord." But Jesus *is* the Lord. Everything He did and said was a message from God. When we read the Gospels, we are listening to the Ultimate Prophet tell us the secrets of the Kingdom.

**8. Answer: B (Jesus is King) Explanation:** This is the theology of **Sovereignty**. If your friend is in charge of the playground, you feel safe. If Jesus is in charge of the *entire universe*, you can feel even safer! Being a King means Jesus has the "final say" over your life, your school, and your future.

**9. Answer: B (The Priest's Sacrifice) Explanation:** In the Old Testament, the **Priest** stood between God and the people. He brought a lamb to pay for sins. Jesus is the "Great High Priest" because He didn't bring a lamb—He *was* the Lamb. He stood between us and God's justice and said, "Take Me instead." Now, He lives in Heaven and constantly prays for you!

## Level 3 Answers: The Rescue

**10. Answer: B (The Great Exchange) Explanation:** This is the heart of **Justification**. Imagine you have a bank account with a trillion dollars of "Debt" (Sin). Jesus has an account with a trillion dollars of "Credit" (Righteousness). On the Cross, He switched accounts with you. He took your debt and gave you His credit. Now, when God looks at your account, He sees Jesus' "Total."

**11. Answer: B (Adoption Security) Explanation:** This is the theology of **Family**. In ancient times, when you were adopted, it was a legal move that could never be undone. God didn't just "rescue" you like a lifeguard; He "adopted" you like a Father. You are a son or daughter of the King. Even when you mess up, you are still His child.

**12. Answer: B (The Body of Christ) Explanation:** This is **Ecclesiology**. The Church is a "Body." If you think you aren't important because you aren't a "pastor" or a "teacher," remember that a body needs its pinky toe just as much as its eyes! Every kid in the church has a job to do, even if it's just being the person who notices who is lonely.

**13. Answer: False Explanation:** The Church is a **People**, not a place. The "Invisible Church" is all believers everywhere. You could have church in a park, in a house, or in a basement. As long as the "called-out ones" are there, the Church is there!

## Level 4 Answers: The Feelings & The Future

**14. Answer: B (Anger as an Alarm) Explanation:** This is the **Theology of Emotions**. God gets "Holy Anger" when He sees people being hurt. He gave us anger so we would want to protect people and stand up for what is right. The problem is our sin turns that "good anger" into "selfish anger." A Junior Theologian asks: "Is my alarm going off for God's reasons or my reasons?"

**15. Answer: B (Gratitude/Tracing) Explanation:** This is the theology of **Beatitude**. God is the source of all joy. When you are happy, don't stop at the "thing" (the toy or the game). Use that thing as a "ladder" to climb up and thank God. This makes your happiness last longer because it connects you to the King!

**16. Answer: B (Glorified Bodies) Explanation:** This is **Eschatology**. The Bible says our "lowly bodies" will be made like Jesus' "glorious body." Imagine your body, but with the "Upgrade" button pressed. No more glasses, no more braces, no more allergies, and no more getting tired! It's a physical resurrection.

**17. Answer: B (The Renewed Earth) Explanation:** Many people think Heaven is a boring cloud-city. But theology teaches us God is making a **New Earth**. We will have a world that is perfect—with mountains to climb, fruit to eat, and work to do—but without any of the bad stuff like thorns, sweat, or sadness. It's "Eden 2.0."


## Level 5 Answers: The Master Class

**18. Answer: B (Omniscience) Explanation:** This is the "Honesty Attribute." Since God already knows your secret, you aren't "hiding" it from Him, you're just hiding *yourself* from His grace. Confessing your sin is just saying "God, You saw that, and I'm sorry." It brings you back into the light.

**19. Answer: A (Justification) Explanation:** This is the "Peace Doctrine." If you feel like God is mad at you, remind yourself that He already "Judged" your sin at the Cross. He isn't a "cranky boss" waiting for you to fail; He is a "Loving Father" who has already declared you Righteous in Christ.

**20. Answer: B (Image-Bearer) Explanation:** This is the "Love Your Neighbor" doctrine. We don't love people because they are "nice." We love them because they belong to God. Treating a mean person with respect is a way of showing honor to the King who made them. It's like being nice to a Prince even if the Prince is having a bad day.

## Final Score Review:

- **15-20 Correct: Master Theologian!** You have a solid grasp of the "System." You are ready to start teaching others how the Bible fits together. Keep studying and keep "Tracing" everything back to God!

- **10-14 Correct: Intermediate Theologian.** You have a great foundation, but some of the "Big Words" are still a bit tricky. Go back and read the "Action Manual" one more time to see how the doctrines fit into your daily life.

- **0-9 Correct: Apprentice Theologian.** You are just getting started! Don't be discouraged: theology is a life-long journey. Pick one attribute of God (like Love or Power) and focus on that for a week.

**Conclusion of the Quiz:** Theology isn't about being "smart"; it's about being "transformed." The reason we learn these things is so we can love God with all our **minds**. Now that you know the Blueprint, go out and live in the House!